Music Theory
Made Easy

Second Revised Edition

By David Harp

© 1994 Musical I. Press, Inc.
P.O. Box 1561
Montpelier, Vermont 05602

ISBN 0 - 918321 - 99 - 9

Book design by Rita Ricketson

Drawings by Don Mayne

Distributed to the music trade
by Music Sales Corporation

Distributed to the book trade
by Publishers Group West

Printed in the United States of America by
Vicks Lithographic and Printing Corporation

musical i press
Montpelier, Vermont

Acknowledgements

Thanks to Charlie Winton, Randy Fleming, and the rest of the crew at Publishers Group West, both for the fun in the good times, and the support in the bad ones. Without PGW, my life and career might now be quite different, indeed.

And also to Kevin Crossett and the Play It Again Sam folk, Marge Bower, Gail England, Ken Levinson, and Michael, Sandy, and Dan Levine for their help, plus Barrie and the Music Sales gang.

And, of course, to Rita and Katie, without whom neither this nor the following books would even exist, or matter.

Other Books by David Harp

Instant Blues Harmonica (Volumes I and II)

Instant Chromatic Harmonica: The Blues/Jazz Improvisation Method

Instant Guitar

Instant Flute

The Instant Harmonica Kit for Kids

Harmonica Positions

The Three Minute Meditator (with Dr. Nina Feldman)

Me and My Harmonica

Instant Blues/Rock Harmonica: The Video

Make Me Musical: Instant Harmonica — A Complete Musical Education for Kids

Metaphysical Fitness (with Dr. Nina Feldman)

The Three Minute Meditator Audiotape

How To Whistle Like A Pro (with Jason Serinus)

Bending the Blues

EarthCards (with the Write For Action Group)

The New Three Minute Meditator

The Instant Rhythm Kit

In Hot Water: How To Save Your Back, Neck, and Shoulders In Ten Minutes A Day (with Dr. Pat Horay)

How To Play Country & Western Harmonica

The Pocket Harmonica Songbook

The Pocket Musician (video)

Better Breathing Through Harmonica

Three Minutes to Blues Harmonica (video)

David is also the founder of *Harmonica America,* a non-profit organization devoted to bringing the benefits of harmonica to people with disabilities, people in nursing homes, and inner city children.

"Whose love of music was immense
Whose love of jamming was intense
Whose love of playing was him at his best."

As remembered by his sister: "Mike could play just about anything. He had a four track tape recorder and a mixer set up in his little studio apartment, as well as a Fender Rhodes piano, three electric guitars, an old drum kit, a drum machine, two or three microphones, and various "percussion instruments" (ranging from old trash cans to sets of drumsticks) strewn around the place. So almost his entire living space was devoted to playing and recording music.

"When friends would drop by, the visit would always turn into a jamm session — it was a lot of fun! Even though many of us couldn't play very well at first, he taught us the basics so that we could all play along — he *never* had an attitude that anybody "wasn't good enough" to play with.

"Mike had exquisite taste in music and knew how to play all the great songs, from Hank Ballard to Buddy Holly to Dylan and the Stones. If there was a new song everybody liked on the radio, he'd figure it out and we'd record it. He'd tell us the chords, and we'd have pads of paper around with chords written all over them — lots of E's and A's and B7's, I remember. Mike would lay down a bass riff with his Fender, someone would play rhythm guitar, and someone else would play drums. Then we'd add lead guitar and vocals. Sometimes the tape player was just set to record and we'd play on and on for hours.

" His knowledge and total joy of music made him a high to be around. Plus he was funny. So we'd be playing music and laughing deep into the night.

"Mike also played and recorded a lot of music when he was alone. I can picture him now, with two huge speakers right next to his ears, volume up loud, listening to something he'd just written, played, and recorded..."

And I can still hear his laughter

And I can still hear his song*.

Barbara Martinelli   Berkeley, California   Fall, 1991

*Dire Straits: *The Man's Too Strong*.

Table of Contents

How to Use This Book

This book is designed to be useful. I want you to be able to use it to get good musical results — quickly! But "useful" often means different things to different people. Some of you will want to know why music theory is the way it is, and how it got that way. Others of you will only want to know the information that helps you to play, right away.

So I've put all of the most important material from the earlier chapters on the science and history of music theory into "boxes", like the one at the end of this section.

Please feel free to read every word in every chapter, if you like, **including every box.** But if you're in a rush, just read the box at the end of each of the beginning sections. Check out every picture, diagram, and section title as you scan through the book for the next box. If you're going from box to box, and find a particular box interesting, go back and read the whole thing. By the way: all words in **"boldface"** are words that you should know, so notice them, whether they are in a box, or not.

And, of course, if you don't understand the material in a box reasonably well, that means that you should probably go back and read through the entire section.

Boxes like this one sum up the material in the section above them. So you can either go on and read the whole next section, or flip your way through to the next box.

Who Is David Harp?

I used to be a self-labelled "musical idiot." Couldn't carry a tune in a bucket, or so I believed. Music theory used to seem incomprehensible to me, as though it were written in Martian.

Once I began to play the harmonica, I realized that I wasn't unmusical at all. But it wasn't until I learned some music theory that I really became a musician. Now I love to play and teach many different instruments. And it's my knowledge of music theory that lets me play almost any instrument and style of music — a little bit — right away!

I'm still studying and learning about music and music theory. So, I'll sometimes use the pronouns "we" and "us" as I talk to you, since we're all in this exciting musical adventure together. Other times, when suggesting that you try something that I can already do, I may use the pronoun "you."

Who Needs this Book?

I believe that every musician, from total first day beginner to pro, needs at least a basic understanding of music theory. Although some people argue that many early greats of blues, rock and jazz music knew no theory, they obviously had an intuitive grasp of how to make music. So if you are a Louis Armstrong or a Little Walter, I suppose you can skip this book. If not...

Knowing music theory will teach you to be able to play and improvise any kind of music. It won't help your playing technique — only practice will do that. If you are a beginning folk guitarist, this book will soon have you able to play (and compose) beginning level blues, country, and rock guitar. If you're a good blues harmonica player, you'll soon be able to play and create good country, rock, folk, and pop harp, too. But how well you play any type of music will depend on your technical command of your instrument.

If you are a complete beginner, make sure that you are using a method of instruction for your chosen instrument that is easy to understand. I'll plug my own instructional methods for blues harp, chromatic harmonica, guitar, block flute, and percussion, on page 78.

This book is designed to be used with any instrument. But if you use an instrument without a visible means of producing notes or chords (harmonica players and vocalists, especially), or if you play an instrument that only produces single notes, like a flute or clarinet, it may be worth your while to buy an inexpensive electronic keyboard or guitar to work with. This will be more important if you want to improvise music, and especially if you would like to compose your own songs. If this interests you, please see the Keyboard/Guitar section, on page 75.

Every musician should know at least the basics of music theory. Vocalists and "single note instrument" players should read the paragraph just above this box.

What <u>Isn't</u> in this Book

Music theory is a big subject. An entire library could be filled with books on it, and graduate students earn Ph.D's by spending years studying a tiny subsection of music theory, such as "use of the flatted fifth note in New Orleans Jazz music from the years 1920 to 1941."

This book won't go into that kind of detail. In 80 pages? No way! I'll only cover what is most important to know when making music, only the practical basics of what us musicians *really* need to know, when playing by ourselves or with others. I will often simplify things (especially in the sections on the history of music theory), but I'll try not to be inaccurate. And I'll try to provide you with a solid general understanding of music theory, that will allow you to go on and use other music theory books to explore specific subjects of interest to you.

Also, most music theory books require that the reader know or learn to read standard musical notation (notes on staff lines). Not this book. While learning how to read standard notation is a valuable skill, it has little to do with understanding and using music theory.

To me, demanding that the musician learn standard notation in order to learn music theory is like demanding that someone learn to speak Chinese before letting them play Chinese Checkers.

I've tried to include only what you really need to know in this book. And I won't force you to learn how "to read music" in standard notation.

What _Is_ in this Book

I'll begin with a discussion of how sounds and musical "notes" are produced. Then I'll tell you how the musical system that we use today was created over the past 2500 years.

Next, we'll study the language used to describe music, and learn the general and specific names that are used to describe notes. Once you understand this language, we'll study scales and chords, the basic building blocks of music.

Then we'll study the way in which chords are put together to create folk, blues, rock, and country music. We'll also study a bit of rhythm, and then learn how to use scales and chords to improvise in any style of music, and to create our own songs. An appendix (page 75) will discuss how to use this material to play — confidently — with other musicians, in public and private.

We'll finish with a very brief study of jazz, the most complex musical form. And with suggestions on where to go when you've finished this book, once you've developed a good basic grasp of music theory.

Do you want a preview now of what you're going to be reading about later? Read the above section — it's probably a good idea, but you don't have to.

About The Upcoming Cassette

Sometime in 1995, an audiotape demonstrating most of the information in this book will be available.

The Science of Sound

As I said earlier, some people like to know *why* things work, before learning how to use them. The following sections will tell you the way in which sound is produced, and how sound is interpreted by the human brain.

Good Vibrations

Imagine a bumblebee that has suffered the indignity of falling into a swimming pool. Its wings vibrate, and these vibrations make tiny waves in the water. These waves would make a leaf near the edge of the pool vibrate at the same speed as the bee's wings are vibrating in the water.

Whenever anything vibrates, it creates additional vibrations that spread through the air. Sometimes what is vibrating is obvious, like the head of a drum or the wings of a mosquito or a guitar string. Sometimes what vibrates is not so obvious, like the air molecules inside a flute, or the reed of a clarinet.

The speed of any of these vibrations will vary, depending on what is vibrating. The drum head vibrates at a low speed, and sends big, slow waves through the air. The mosquito's wings vibrate at a high speed, and send tiny, fast waves vibrating through the air.

Likewise, in any musical instrument, the size of the vibrating object affects the vibratory speed. For instance, the larger, heavier strings in the "low end" of a guitar or a piano vibrate more slowly than the smaller, lighter strings in the "high end". We'll consider "low" and "high" sounds in a moment. But no matter the speed of the vibrations, the vibrations radiate out into the air from the vibrating object, and make the air itself vibrate.

Air, Ear, and Brain

When vibrations travelling in the air reach our eardrums, our eardrums then vibrate at the same speed as whatever is vibrating, just like the vibrations traveling in the water from the bee's wings made the leaf vibrate.

A complicated set of bones and organs inside our ears change the vibrations that strike our eardrums into electrical messages. Nerves then carry these electrical messages to our brain.

When our eardrums are vibrating **slowly**, our brain receives a "slow vibration" electrical message, and it interprets this message as what we call a **"low"** sound. When our eardrums are vibrating **quickly**, our brain is sent a "fast vibration" electrical message, and it interprets this message as what we call a **"high"** sound. Thus hearing is an interaction which occurs among three parts: the vibrations in the air, the ear, and the brain.

The human brain can interpret messages when the eardrum is vibrating as slow as 20 vibrations per second, and as fast as 20,000 vibrations per seconds. The lowest note on a piano vibrates our eardrum at about 27 vibrations per second, and the highest note on the piano vibrates our eardrum at about 4,000 vibrations per second.

Vibration causes sound. As the speed of a vibration **increases**, the sound that we hear becomes **higher**. As the speed of a vibration **decreases**, the sound becomes **lower**.

Pitch and Note

The highness or lowness of a sound is called the **"pitch"** of that sound. Let's choose a particular vibrational speed, like 260 vibrations per second, for example. Anything vibrating at the speed of 260 vibrations per second will always produce a sound with a specific pitch. As long as the speed of vibration remains the same, the note has the same pitch. For convenience, we can abbreviate **"vibrations per second"** as **"vps."**

A sound produced by any particular vibrational speed, whether it is vibrating at 260 vps, or 351 vps, or 1234 vps, or 2345 vps, or any other speed from 20 to 20,000 vps, is called a **"note."**

If we like, we can call the difference between a lower note and a higher note the **"musical distance"** between them, although the more correct term for this musical distance is **"interval."** A person with a well-trained ear can hear the difference between notes as close as those produced, for example, by 260 vps and 261 or 262 vps. Even an untrained person can tell the difference between notes as close together as those produced by 260 vps and 265 or 270 vps.

The highness or lowness of a sound is called the **"pitch"** of that sound. A sound produced by any particular vibrational speed is called a **"note."** The difference between any two notes can be called the **"musical distance"** or the **"interval"** between them.

Octave Notes and Octave Distance

Let's take a note vibrating at a particular speed, such as 260 vps, and double the speed of vibration to 520 vps (260 x 2 = 520). Comparing the two sounds (260 vps and 520 vps), we'll find that they sound remarkably alike, although the faster vibration sound is obviously higher.

If we double the speed of vibration once again (520 x 2 = 1040 vps), we find that all three sounds (260 vps, 520 vps and 1040 vps) bear a great similarity to each other. Likewise the sounds produced by 300 vps, 600 vps and 1200 vps sound alike, and so on.

Doubling the speed of vibration of a particular sound will always produce a new sound that seems to repeat the sound quality of the first one, only higher. We call these similar notes **"octave notes."** We can also call the musical distance between two of these octave notes **"one octave."**

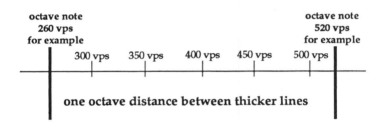

one octave distance between thicker lines

It is very easy to hear that two octave notes are similar in sound, even though one is higher than the other. In fact, scientists have shown that if you train a dog to salivate when it hears a lower octave note (like 260 vps), the dog will also salivate when it hears a higher octave note (like 520 vps). But, surprisingly, the dog *won't* drool when it hears a note of 240 vps or 280 vps! Even dogs can recognize that octave notes are somehow almost "the same."

If we take a note vibrating at a particular speed, like 100 vibrations per second, and double it (200 vibrations per second), both notes will sound very much alike. Notes vibrating twice or half as fast as each other are called **"octave notes."** The musical distance (also called the **"interval"**) between two octave notes is called **"one octave."**

Breaking Up the Octave Distance

Octave notes are pretty far apart, in musical distance terms. An untrained person can easily tell the difference between a note produced by 100 vps and 105 vps. So there is clearly room to fit many notes in the octave distance — that is, room to fit many notes in between a note vibrating at 100 vps and its higher octave note vibrating at 200 vps.

Breaking the octave distance into smaller and more usable parts is called **"creating a scale."** The word **"scale"** refers to a particular way of dividing that octave distance into pieces.

Every known human culture recognizes octave notes, and has some organized way of creating a scale by breaking up the octave distance. In China, the octave distance is broken into five parts to create a Chinese scale. In India, the octave distance is broken into 22 parts to create an Indian scale. The following section describes how a Greek scale developed 2500 years ago has provided Western Culture with the scales that we still use today.

Breaking the octave distance into smaller and more usable parts is called **"creating a scale."** Every known human culture recognizes octave notes, and has some organized way of breaking up the octave distance — that is, some way of creating a scale.

A Brief History of Music

One of humankind's first musical instruments, and the great-great-granddaddy of all stringed instruments, was the hunting bow. Many thousands of years ago, hunters discovered that the "plunk" sound of the bowstring changed depending on whether the string was stretched more tightly or more loosely. You can demonstrate this for yourself, by plucking a rubber band once, then stretching it more and plucking it again.

Aboriginal peoples around the world still use the hunting bow to make music, today. They simply place one end of the bow on the ground, and lean on the top of the bow to stretch or loosen the bowstring as they pluck it. The effect is something like a one-stringed bass fiddle, or a jug band's washtub bass.

Pythagoras The Greek!

2500 years ago the brilliant Greek mathematician Pythagoras began to wonder why a bow string produces different sounds when stretched to different lengths. He soon discovered that lengths of string stretched between two points with equal tension would produce varying sounds, depending on the length of the string.

Pythagoras began to experiment with the sounds produced by plucking different lengths of string. He noticed that if he plucked two strings simultaneously when one was exactly half as long as the other, they would both produce sounds that somehow seemed very similar, even though the shorter string made a sound that was clearly higher.

Modern musicians now know that the "half-as-long" string was vibrating exactly twice as fast as the longer string, and thus the shorter string was producing an octave note which sounded very much like the longer string's original note. But the vibrational nature of sound was not discovered until nearly 1700 A.D., so Pythagoras had only the relative lengths of the strings, and the evidence of his own ears, to base his research on.

The ancient Greeks loved mathematics, and enjoyed using ratios (the relationship between two numbers) in their architecture and in their art. For example, the ratio of the height of a statue's head to the length of the body was 7 to 1. The ratio of a building's width to its height was often 3 to 2. So it was natural for Pythagoras to want to apply similar mathematical ratios to his musical experimentation.

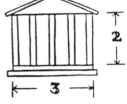

Pythagoras* reasoned that if the mathematical ratio of 2 to 1 (one string twice as long as the other) would produce two notes that seemed so similar, perhaps other simple ratios like 3 to 2, or 4 to 3, could be applied to the lengths of vibrating strings to produce more notes that somehow "related well" to each other.

* Pythagoras may actually have been more than one person, confusing though that sounds. And, by the way, much of my version of the history of music has been contracted and simplified, in order to make sense of what came later. Since no one really knows what went on in the days of Pythagoras, I feel justified in doing this, if it helps to explain why we do what we do now, which it does!

The Chromatic Scale

Pythagoras continued his experimentation. He used a variety of mathematical ratios (like 5 to 4, 3 to 2, 4 to 3, etc.) to divide up the musical distance between two octave notes into smaller sections. Eventually he ended up by dividing each octave into 12 equal sections.

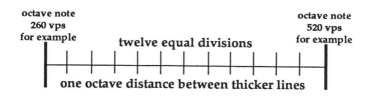

As I said, breaking up the octave distance into a number of smaller pieces is called "creating a scale". Pythagoras' 12 note division, called the **"chromatic scale,"** is still the basic scale used by most of our Western civilization's music and musical instruments.

Why did he do it this way? No one knows, but a quick look at one octave of a piano keyboard (which usually contains seven and one third chromatic scales next to each other) shows that Pythagoras' 12 note octave division has stood the test of time!

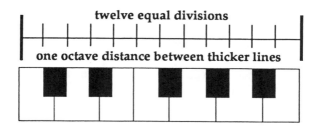

By about the year 500 B.C., the Greek scientist Pythagoras created a scale by breaking the musical distance between two octave notes into 12 equal parts. This 12 note scale, called the "chromatic scale," still forms the basis for all of our culture's music.

After learning the different names used to describe the twelve notes of Pythagoras' **chromatic scale,** we will learn how these twelve notes are used to produce the blues, rock, folk, country, jazz, classical, and pop music that we hear and play today!

Naming the Notes

Pythagoras created the chromatic scale, but as far as we know today, he did not give names to its notes. Yet without names, it was hard to describe a particular note of the chromatic scale. So, over time, various ways were developed to give names to notes.

By approximately the year 500 A.D., Boethius used the letters of the Roman alphabet to give each note a name. By the end of the 12th century A.D., the Benedictine monk Guido D'Arezzo was using symbols placed on lines to name notes.

Today we still use ways of note-naming based on the methods of Boethius and Guido D'Arrezzo. A number of newer systems of note names also exist — in fact, so many that it can be very confusing!

One of the biggest problems facing the beginning music theory student is that there are so many different ways of referring to the same note. But we'll study each way, and see that it's not as confusing as it looks at first!

There are two main ways of giving names to notes. We will study **"specific note names"** first, then study **"general note names."**

Specific note names refer to particular notes. A specific note name refers both to any note vibrating at a certain specific speed (like 100 vps), and its octave notes (those vibrating twice or half as fast, like 50 vps, 200 vps, 400 vps, etc). Confused? Read about Letter Names of Notes, below.

Letter Names of Notes

As more technologically advanced musical instruments, like the piano, were invented and refined using the chromatic scale, the need for a standardized system of note names grew. By the late middle ages, each note on the piano had been given a letter name, using the letters of the English alphabet from A to G. The same name is used for all octaves of that note.

So, for instance, the letter name C is given to the note vibrating at the speed of approximately 260 vibrations per second. The letter C is also used to name the note vibrating half as fast (130 vps), and twice as fast (520 vps). The same letter C is used to describe all of the C octave notes on the piano. Likewise, the letter A refers to a note vibrating at approximately 220 vps, as well as its other octave A notes like 110 vps and 440 vps.

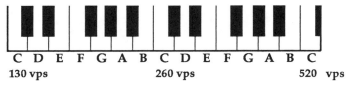

| C | D | E | F | G | A | B | C | D | E | F | G | A | B | C |
130 vps · · · 260 vps · · · 520 vps

As we can see, the letters A to G only name seven of the twelve notes of the chromatic scale. On the piano, these are the white notes. But the black notes that fall in between the white notes need names, also.

The white notes of the piano keyboard each have a letter name, from A to G. Octave notes share the same letter name.

Sharp Names (#) and Flat Names (b)

Each white note of the piano is indicated by a single letter. **But each black note has two names.** And this is where many of us (me included, for a long time) get lost. So take a deep breath, and read on...

One "black note name" is called a **"sharp"** name. Sharp means **"higher than."** The sharp name tells us which white note a black note is a little bit **higher** than. So the black note named "A sharp" is the black note a little bit higher than A. Sometimes instead of using the word "sharp," we use the symbol **#**.

The other letter name is called a **"flat"** name. Flat means **"lower than"**. The flat name tells us which white key the black key is a little bit lower than. So the black key named "B flat" is the black key a little bit lower than B. Sometimes instead of the word "flat", we use the symbol **b**.

If these sharp and flat names seem confusing, think about these three houses. If you were describing how to find **your house** to a visitor coming from further **up** the hill, you might say, "My house is a bit *lower than* Smith's house." If you were describing it to someone coming from **down** the hill, you'd say, "My house is a bit *higher than* Jones' house." Same exact house, but two different ways to describe it, depending on which direction the visitor is coming from.

Like the house in the story, each black note has two names. When we think about the black note between A and B in terms of the A, we can call it A sharp. When we think about that same black note in terms of B, we can call it B flat. It really doesn't make much difference which one we use, as long as we know that it's the same note, no matter *what* we call it!

Here are two ways to write the names of the notes of the chromatic scale, going from A to G, and including sharp and flat notes. One line uses only sharp note names, the other uses only flat note names.

A	A#	B	C	C#	D	D#	E	F	F#	G	G#

A	Bb	B	C	Db	D	Eb	E	F	Gb	G	Ab

Notice that there is not a sharp or flat note in between each non-sharp or flat note, just as there is not a black note in between each of the piano keys.

Each black note of the piano has *two* names, a **sharp (#)** note name and a **flat (b)** note name. If you don't already know about these two ways of refering to the same note, you had better read the entire preceding section.

$$A\# = Bb$$

Study this picture of the notes of two octaves of a piano. The black notes of the first octave are labelled with sharp names, and the black notes of the second octave are labelled with flat names.

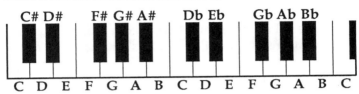

When I refer to one of these black notes on the piano, I may call it by just a single note name — *either* its sharp name or its flat name. Or sometimes I will call one black note by *both* names. For instance, I may call the black note between the D and E notes by the name **"D#/Eb."** Or I may write it as **"D# or Eb."** Make sure that you know what I mean when you see this: **It's important!**

$$D\#/Eb$$

There are some general rules for when to use the sharp name of a note, and when to use the flat name of that note. But these rules are not important now, so we'll wait to discuss them. In fact, these rules are mostly important only if you plan to read and write standard notation. So just make sure you understand that A# is the same note as Bb, C# is the same as Db, and so on, and you'll be in good shape!

Playing a Chromatic Scale

We can begin a chromatic scale by choosing *any* note of a piano, and then just playing up or down twelve notes (regardless of whether they are black or white). This will bring us back to the "same" note we started on, one octave distance higher or lower.

Here are two examples of chromatic scales, marked off by the upper and lower brackets in the picture below. One begins on an E note and ends on an E. The other begins on an A# (A sharp) note, and ends on an Bb (which is the same note as A#, right?). Can you read off the twelve notes of a chromatic scale beginning on the note C? Beginning on the note F#?

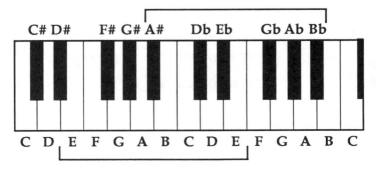

Now would be a good time to practice playing some different chromatic scales, like those above, on the instrument of your choice. If you're a vocalist, you may want to record some keyboard chromatic scales, and try to sing along, matching them note for note.

The Concept of Key

Whenever we choose a note to begin a scale on, the letter name of that beginning note is then the **"key"** of that scale. So the chromatic scale beginning and ending on the note E is called an E chromatic scale, or a chromatic scale in the key of E. The scale beginning and ending on the note Bb is called **"a Bb chromatic scale"** or **"a chromatic scale in the key of Bb."**

When we choose a specific note to begin a scale on, the name of that beginning note is the "key" of that scale. For example, a chromatic scale that begins on the note D is called a **"D chromatic scale"** or a **"chromatic scale in the key of D"**.

Standard Notation Note Names

The symbols that Guido D'Arezzo placed on lines to indicate specific notes eventually developed into today's standard musical notation, also known simply as **"standard notation."**

In standard notation, note symbols of different kinds are used to indicate how long that note should be held. Where the note symbol is placed on the lines (which are called the **"staff"**) indicates the note's pitch.

One staff, called the treble clef, is used for high notes. Another, called the bass clef, is used for low notes. A line in between the two clefs is called "middle C," and represents the note in the middle of the piano keyboard. Below are some treble clef notes.

A sharp symbol (#) or flat symbol (b) before a note on the staff indicates that this note should actually be a "black" note on the piano, since the lines and spaces only represent the letter names A B C D E F and G.

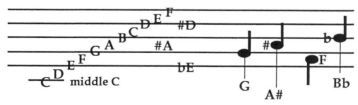

As I've said, learning to read standard notation can be very useful for the musician. It enables us to reproduce exactly any piece of music that another musician has taken the trouble to write down.

However, reading standard notation has little to do with learning music theory, so I do not require or teach it in this book.

Tablature Note Names

Sometimes notation for a particular instrument is written in **"tablature"** form. Tablature requires neither a knowledge of letter names nor standard notation names. Many instruments have tablature notation systems, and the system used is different for each instrument. **"Tab,"** as it is sometimes called, is easy to use, but often people who play by tab neglect to learn music theory, and thus limit themselves to playing only what other instrumentalists have written out in tablature form. There are many varieties of tablature for each musical instrument. I'll demonstrate the tab systems that I use in my instructional methods for harmonica, flute, and guitar.

For instance, my harmonica tablature tells you which of the harmonica's ten holes to breathe through, and whether to breathe in or out. The number represents the number of the correct hole, and the In or the Out tells you whether to inhale or exhale on that hole.

Oh	when	the	saints
4	5	5	6
out	out	in	out

In guitar tablature, the number tells you which of the guitar frets to put your finger on. The line that the number is placed on tells you which string to pluck as your finger is pushes down on the indicated fret.

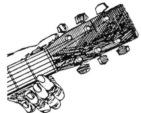

```
          Oh      when     the    saints
E ────────────────────────────────────────
B ────────────────────────────────────────
G ────────────────────────────────────────
D ──────────────────────────────0──────2──
A ────────0────────────4───────────────────
E ────────────────────────────────────────
```

My flute tablature tells you how many of the "fipple-style" flute's six holes should be covered up by your fingertips.

Oh	when	the	saints
6	4	3	2

If you've ever wanted to play harmonica, guitar, drums, or flute, please read about my "instant results" instructional methods, on page 78.

General Note Names

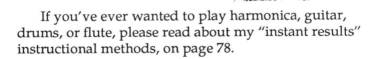

Specific note names refer to particular notes. General note names refer to *relationships* between notes. The two common general ways of naming notes are **"solmi"** names and **"roman numeral"** names.

Think about the general and specific names we use for people. We'll use the Smith and Jones families, from page 17's picture, for examples. Consider this:

We can use *general* names for people in our family, like "me" and "mother" and "father" and "daughter." We can also use *specific* names for these people. I am "David." My mother's name is "Frieda." My father's name is "Fred." My daughter's name is "Katie."

The specific names — David, Frieda, Fred, and Katie — refer to specific, particular people. The general names — me, mother, father, and daughter — refer to the *relationships* between those people. Let's look at some general and specific names:

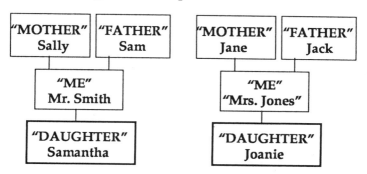

But here's an important point: Once you know who "me" is, you then can figure out specifically who "mother," "father," or "daughter" is.

In other words, once we say that we're talking about Mr. Smith, it's easy to figure out that "mother" means "Sally Smith," that "Father" means "Sam Smith," and "Daughter" means "Samantha Smith."

Likewise, once we say that we are talking about Mrs. Jones — That the general name "me" has been given temporarily to "Mrs. Jones" — then the general names "mother," "father" and "daughter" can be instantly translated to refer to specific people in Mrs. Jones' life: Parents Jane and Jack, daughter Joanie.

In the same way, the specific note names that we have learned, like the letter names of notes, refer to specific, particular, notes. When I read the note name "F#" I know just what note of the chromatic scale the writer is refering to. Reading "F#" is like reading the name "Sam Smith." A specific note, a specific person.

But the general note names described below refer to the *relationships* between notes, just as the general names "me" and "mother" and "father" and "daughter" refer to the relationships between people in our lives. Please keep my examples in mind as you read more about general ways of refering to musical notes.

If the following section on Solmization seems at all confusing, please don't stop. It *will* become clearer. Just go on and read the sections on Roman numeral names, and on using The NoteFinder™. This will help to clarify the concept of general note names...

Solmization Note Names

One general way of naming notes is called **"solmization."** It's a less useful general way to name notes than the roman numeral names I describe below, but perhaps easier to understand, at first.

These "solmi" names tend to be used by vocalists more than instrumentalists, and more in Europe than in the United States — they are a great way of communicating with non-English speaking musicians!

In solmi, each of the twelve notes of the chromatic scale, in order, is given a syllable name, instead of a letter name, like this (the second DO starts a new scale.)

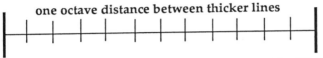

one octave distance between thicker lines

DO di RE ri ME FA fi SO si LA li TI (DO)

You are probably already familiar with a shortened version of these solmi names, which I will describe in more detail in the section on the major scale.

DO   RE   ME FA   SO   LA   TI DO

Syllable names don't refer to specific letter name notes — *Unless* we say what note we want the syllable DO to refer to. Just as I said before: The general name "mother" doesn't refer to a specific person until we say that "me" means "Mr. Jones" — Then we automatically know that "mother" means "Jane Jones."

The specific letter name note that each solmi syllable refers to depends on which letter name note we choose to use for DO, just as the name of each individual in the previous example depends on who we mean by the word "me."

For instance: Look at the chart below. Let's say that we are using the note "C" as our DO. (This is like saying that we are using "Mr. Smith" as our "me.") We can then automatically see that C# must be di, D must be RE, D# must be ri, and so on. (This is like saying that once we know that "me" means Mr. Smith, it's easy to figure out that "mother" means "Sally," that "Father" means "Sam," and that "Daughter" means "Samantha.")

If we decide that we want G to be our DO, then G# would be di, A would be RE, and so on. This is like saying that once we decide that "me" means Mrs. Jones, we then know that "mother" means "Jane," that "Father" means "Jack," and that "Daughter" means "Joanie." Get the idea?

DO	di	RE	ri	ME	FA	fi	SO	si	LA	li	TI	DO
C	C#	D	D#	E	F	F#	G	G#	A	A#	B	C
G	G#	A	A#	B	C	C#	D	D#	E	F	F#	G

All other chromatic scales in every key, D# and Bb, F and A and E, can be related to the solmization names in the same way. Just decide what letter name note you want to be your "DO" (F#, for example), write out each one of the rest of the chromatic scale notes in order until you return to F#, and you will see how the other solmi names relate to the letter names of your new chromatic scale in the key of F#.

So as you can see, solmi names are not as specific as letter names. They do not refer to particular notes, but they do accurately describe the relationship between notes, that is, the musical distances between them. They do this by describing the *position* of a note within the chromatic scale, and its relationship to the other notes of that chromatic scale.

For instance, a DO note is always the first note of a chromatic scale, no matter what specific note you may choose to start on. A di note is always the second note of a chromatic scale, and one note up from a DO note on the piano keyboard.

Thus the third note of the E chromatic scale and the third note of the Bb chromatic scale indicated by brackets above are called by the same solmi name: RE. This is true even though the specific letter name of the third note of the E chromatic scale is F# (or Gb), and the specific letter name of the third note of the Bb chromatic scale is C. A si note is always the ninth note of a chromatic scale, and a LA note will always be the tenth note of any chromatic scale (counting black and white keys as exactly the same). This gives us a convenient way of referring to the *position* of a note in the chromatic scale, no matter what particular key scale we are talking about.

Just as in any chromatic scale, all DO notes are exactly one octave apart, and sound very similar to each other. All RE notes are one octave apart, and every RE sounds similar to every other RE. This picture may help to illustrate for you the repetitive nature of the chromatic scale.

By the way: This is hard stuff, so don't feel bad if it seems difficult — It should! Just go back and re-read my examples, then go on to the next type of general note names: Roman Numerals.

Roman Numeral Names

There is one other, more commonly used way of referring to notes. It is very similar to the solmi names, but instead of being given a syllable, each note of the chromatic scale is given a roman numeral. Only seven roman numerals (I, II, III, IV, V, VI, and VII) are used, so five sharp or flat signs are added to make the twelve note names needed for a chromatic scale. Since any note with a sharp name also has a flat name, I'll write the roman numeral names twice — with sharp names first, and then underneath with flat names.

I	I#	II	II#	III	IV	IV#	V	V#	VI	VI#	VII	I
I	bII	II	bIII	III	IV	bV	V	bVI	VI	bVII	VII	I

Sharp signs (#) can come before or after Roman numerals, but flats (b) almost always come before. Confusingly, when writing letter note names, the flat sign usually comes after the letter, as in Bb or Eb!

Once again, these roman numeral names are general ways of describing the *relationships* between different notes. It will help if you understand my "me - mother - father - daughter" analogy on page 21, and how it relates to the solmi names, before you continue.

Comparing Solmi and Roman Names

The chart below shows how the solmization and roman note (# names only) compare to each other.

DO	di	RE	ri	ME	FA	fi	SO	si	LA	li	TI	DO
I	I#	II	II#	III	IV	IV#	V	V#	VI	VI#	VII	I

Following are two examples (C and Bb) of how different key chromatic scales correspond to the roman numeral names. Although I have used sharp names for the roman numerals, I will use flat names for the Bb (B flat) scale, just to help you learn and remember that each "black note" has two names. I could've written out the Bb scale as an A# (A sharp) scale, using the same notes but different names.

I	I#	II	II#	III	IV	IV#	V	V#	VI	VI#	VII	I
C	C#	D	D#	E	F	F#	G	G#	A	A#	B	C
Bb	B	C	Db	D	Eb	E	F	Gb	G	Ab	A	Bb

Pronounciation of Roman Names

Roman numeral names are usually pronounced as "first," "fourth," "sixth," and so on. If a flat or sharp sign is used, they are usually pronounced as "sharped fourth," "flatted seventh," and so on. Occasionally they are called "sharp second" or "flat seventh."

Why Use Roman Numeral Names?

Just as with the solmization names, the roman numeral names provide us with a convenient way to describe the relationship between notes, without using specific letter names. This will be clearer after I have demonstrated how roman numeral names can help you to figure out the notes of scales and chords, and even tell you which chords to use — so please be patient! Right now we'll use these names to refer to notes, although they are also used to refer to chords

Roman numeral names for notes provide a convenient, general, way to describe the notes of any chromatic scale. Review the examples above, to see how each roman numeral name corresponds to a note in a particular position in the chromatic scale.

A Brief Warning

From now on, I will be using roman numeral names to refer to notes. Since the "I" (roman numeral "one") symbol looks just like the "I" (word meaning "David Harp" in this book), you will have to decide whether I'm talking about the first note of a scale, or about myself, sometimes. I talk about both, quite a bit!

Latin Note Names

There is one more way of speaking about note names that is sometimes used by musicians. As though solmization names and roman numeral names were not enough, musicians sometimes refer to notes by latin names that originated in the Dark Ages.

Fortunately, only three of these names are commonly used. They are pronounced just as they look, and I will discuss how they are used in playing situations later on. But learn 'em, since they are apt to pop up at the jamm session, although usually as names for types of chords rather than notes, as I'll explain later.

The name **"tonic note"** can be used to refer to the first note of a chromatic scale, the same note which we have already called the DO or roman numeral I note.

The name **"subdominant note"** can be used to refer to the sixth note of a chromatic scale, the same note which we have already called the FA or the roman numeral IV note.

The name **"dominant note"** can be used to refer to the eighth note of a chromatic scale, the same note which we have already called the SO or the roman numeral V note.

About the NoteFinder™

The device that I invented called The NoteFinder™ may help you both to understand the concept of general note names, and, with just a minute or two or practice, to locate the names of any scale or chord that you choose. Make one now, as described.

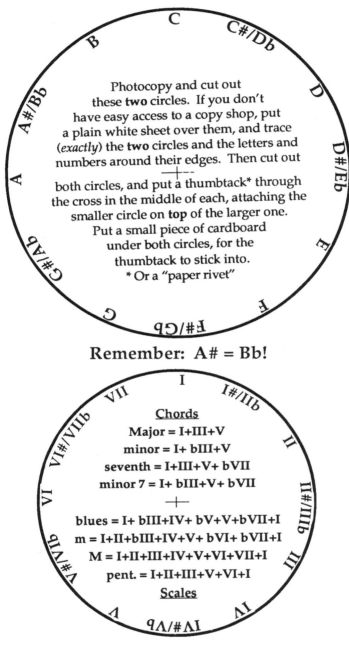

Photocopy and cut out these **two** circles. If you don't have easy access to a copy shop, put a plain white sheet over them, and trace (*exactly*) the **two** circles and the letters and numbers around their edges. Then cut out both circles, and put a thumbtack* through the cross in the middle of each, attaching the smaller circle on **top** of the larger one. Put a small piece of cardboard under both circles, for the thumbtack to stick into.
* Or a "paper rivet"

Remember: A# = Bb!

Chords

Major = I+III+V
minor = I+ bIII+V
seventh = I+III+V+ bVII
minor 7 = I+ bIII+V+ bVII

blues = I+ bIII+IV+ bV+V+bVII+I
m = I+II+bIII+IV+V+ bVI+ bVII+I
M = I+II+III+IV+V+VI+VII+I
pent. = I+II+III+V+VI+I

Scales

To use the NoteFinder™, line up the roman numeral I on the inner circle so that it is directly below the letter C on the outer circle. You'll see that each note of the C chromatic scale is now matched with its roman numeral equivalent: C = I, C#/Db = I#/IIb, D = II, F#/Gb = IV#/Vb, A = VI, and so on throughout the scale. Notice that I have used sharp/flat names for both the roman numeral names and the letter names: Please try not to let this confuse you!

The NoteFinder™ in Use

Now line the roman numeral I on the inner circle up beneath a new letter on the outer circle, like G. Here is what you should see, if you've made your notefinder correctly!

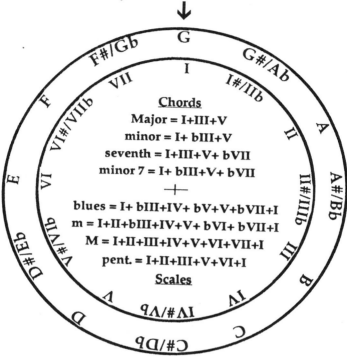

Each roman numeral now corresponds to a new letter name, and you can read off the notes of the G chromatic scale: G = I, G#/Ab = I#/IIb, A = II, and so on. Want to know the sharped fourth of the G chromatic scale? Just look above the IV#/Vb symbol of the inner circle, to see the letter name C#/Db which is closest to IV#/Vb, if not perfectly aligned.

As you can see, the general names of the roman numeral system can be used to show the relationships between notes, once you choose the first note, or key, of the scale that you want to work with. In the next sections, I will show you how to use the NoteFinder™ to find the notes of any chord or scale.

Read this section and make a NoteFinder™, if you want a very useful musical tool, for free!

The End of the Boxes

From now on, you should read the entire book, not just the boxes. The rest of the book is composed of material that should be studied *and* played, on the instrument of your choice. All of the scales, chords, and chord structures are simple enough to be mastered by even a beginning musician, so get out your axe, turn those pages, and wail!

Scales: Musical Alphabets

Pythagoras' twelve note chromatic scale forms the basis for most of today's music, but it is far from the only scale. Many different types of scales are *based on* the chromatic scale, and each of these scales is used to create a different kind of music.

In a way, we might consider a scale to be a kind of "musical alphabet". By using various combinations of the 26 letters of the English alphabet we create English words, sentences, paragraphs and books. By using the letters of the Russian alphabet we create Russian words, sentences and long dreary novels.

Likewise, the notes of any particular culture's scale, be it a Greek scale, a Chinese scale, or a Martian scale, can be put together in various combinations to create music with a sound characteristic of that culture.

If we want, for instance, to play blues music — we must learn to make tasteful combinations of the six notes of the Afro-American blues scale. If we want to improvise country & western music, we will use various combinations of the five notes of the pentatonic scale.

In the following sections we will explore the four most commonly used scales of this culture: the major scale, the minor scale, the blues scale, and the pentatonic scale.

Ha — I fooled you — another box! Remember: You've got to play these scales on the next pages — don't just read about them!

Simplifying the Chromatic Scale

Pythagoras' chromatic scale is rarely used in its complete twelve note form. Instead, certain notes are chosen from it (usually five, six, or seven out of the twelve) to form less complex new scales. We'll find that the general ways of naming notes are very convenient for showing us which of the chromatic scale notes to use, and which to leave out, when playing these new scales.

In the years after Pythagoras invented the chromatic scale, many new seven note scales were experimented with (see page 73 for more on this, if you're interested). They were called **"modes"**, or modal scales. The first of the modal scales was probably what we now call the "major scale." The other modal scales, or modes, were probably based on this "major mode" or "major scale," which I will describe in great detail below.

By the Middle Ages, two of these new modal scales had become far more popular than any of the others that had been tried. These two most popular scales are now called the **"major"** and **"minor"** scales, although they were originally known as the *Ionian* and *Aeolian* modes. Each has seven notes. But the way that each of these two scale's octave distance is broken up is different. Thus the major and minor scales have a very different musical "feel" from each other.

The Major Scale

The major scale eventually evolved as the basis for much of Northern and Western Europe's music. We might call it the "musical alphabet" for most German and English classical music, and some folk music too.

There are twelve possible major scales, one beginning on each note of the chromatic scale, and each named after that note, like C major scale, A major scale, D# major scale, and so on.

The major scale tends to have a strong, brassy, bouncy feel to it. Even random playing of the major scale notes sounds good to us — because these notes are the most basic building blocks of our American musical heritage.

Following, after a bit more discussion, are the solmi and roman ways of describing the notes of the major scale. You will see that unlike the evenly spaced notes of the chromatic scale, the notes of the major scale, and the notes of the minor and blues scales on the next pages, are *not* evenly spaced. And the differences in the way that the notes are spaced in these major, minor, and blues scales makes each one sound excitingly different!

What Major Notes to Use (General)?

How's that? Well, we can see that the major scale uses the notes I, II, III, IV, V, VI, VII, and then ends on the I again. The major scale leaves out the chromatic scale notes I# or IIb, II# or IIIb, IV# or Vb, V# or VIb, and VI# or VIIb. Please look at this diagram comparing the chromatic and major scales, written using both the solmi and the roman numeral names. In the first two lines, I've crossed out the notes that are not used in the major scale. In the last two lines, you can see the "distances" between the notes. For example, ME and FA (III and IV) or TI and DO (VII and I) are closer together, musically and in my chart, than other notes.

DO	di	RE	ri	ME	FA	fi	SO	si	LA	li	TI	DO
I	I#	II	II#	III	IV	IV#	V	V#	VI	VI#	VII	I
DO		RE		ME	FA		SO		LA		TI	DO
I		II		III	IV		V		VI		VII	I

Scale "Formulas"

We might consider the solmi or roman numeral ways of describing the notes of the major scale to be a kind of "formula" for the major scale. They tell us which notes of the chromatic scale to include, and which to leave out. These "scale formulas" are used on the Notefinder™, which will allow you to instantly write out any kind of scale in any specific key.

The "Major Scale Formula"

After we look at the chromatic scale notes that are left out of the major scale, we see that we might write the "major scale formula" as:

I I# II II# III IV IV# V V# VI VI# VII I

I + II + III + IV + V + VI + VII + I

Here are three examples of specific major scales, one beginning on C, one on A# (using sharp names), and one on Eb (using flat names). I'll write out the "major scale formula" on top, then underneath I will write out a chromatic scale beginning on each of the three notes we have chosen to use as the first note of our new major scale.

Once again, I've crossed out the "extra" chromatic scale notes that we do not use in these major scales. So the notes that are not crossed out are the notes of our major scales in these three keys, C, A#, and Eb!

I	+	II	+	III	+ IV	+	V	+	VI	+	VII	+ I
C	C#	D	D#	E	F	F#	G	G#	A	A#	B	C
A#	B	C	C#	D	D#	E	F	F#	G	G#	A	A#
Eb	E	F	Gb	G	Ab	A	Bb	B	C	Db	D	Eb

From now on, I will leave out the "extra" chromatic notes when I write out a scale, instead of leaving them in and crossing them out.

By the way: It's not terribly important, but when writing out specific major scales using letter names, major scales in the keys of G, A, B, C, D, and E are usually written using all sharp (#) names for the notes that need to be sharped or flatted. But the major scale written in the key of F is usually written using the flat (b) name for the one note that must be sharped or flatted (in the case of the F major scale, this means the note Bb).

Major scales starting on notes that are sharp or flat (like the Eb major scale, or the D# major scale) will generally use either all sharp or all flat names, depending on whether you use a sharp name or a flat name for the first note of that scale. So to write out the notes of a Bb major scale, you'd use all flat names, and for the notes of an A# major scale, you'd use all sharp names. Same notes, same scale, but different names.

The Minor Scale

The minor scale evolved as the basis for much of Eastern Europe's music. It has a more plaintive quality than the major scale, and we might consider it to be the alphabet of most Gypsy and Yiddish music, and some folk music as well. A minor scale can be based on each note of the chromatic scale, and will carry that note's name, like the C minor scale, or the Gb minor scale. There are three variations of the minor scale. The one that follows is the most commonly used one, and is called the **"natural minor"** scale. The others will be discussed in the jazz section, on page 74.

Although based on the chromatic scale just as the major scale is, the minor scale uses some of the same notes as the major scale, and some different ones. The minor scale uses the notes I, II, IIIb, IV, V, VIb, and VIIb, then ends on the I again. The minor scale leaves out the chromatic scale notes I# or IIb, III, IV# or Vb, VI, and VII.

Please look at this next diagram comparing the chromatic and minor scales, written using solmi and roman numeral names.

Please notice that instead of crossing out the "extra" notes, I've just omitted the chromatic scale notes that are not used in the minor scale. I will use flat names for the roman names of the minor scale notes, because people tend to think of the minor scale as using flatted thirds, flatted sixths, and flatted sevenths, rather than sharped seconds, sharped fifths, and sharped sixths.

Do	RE	ri	FA	SO	si	li	DO
I	II	bIII	IV	V	bVI	bVII	I

The "Minor Scale Formula"

Below is the minor scale formula, plus three examples of specific minor scales, one written in the key of C minor, one in A minor, and one in Db minor. The key of A minor is considered an easy key in which to play minor scales on keyboard instruments — the white notes from A to G are already spaced right for playing a minor scale, so you don't need to use any of the black keys on the keyboard!

I +	II	+ bIII	+ IV	+ V	+ bVI	+ bVII	+ I
C	D	Eb	F	G	Ab	Bb	C
A	B	C	D	E	F	G	A
Db	Eb	E	Gb	Ab	A	B	Db

The Blues Scale

The mingling of the European musical tradition with the African musical tradition resulted in the creation of the Afro-American **"blues scale."** Its six notes always sound "bluesy" when played together in any combination. Like the major and minor scales, a blues scale can begin on any of the twelve notes of the chromatic scale, so there are twelve possible blues scales, each one named after the note it begins on, like Bb blues scale, or blues scale in the key of F.

Blues scale notes are traditionally referred to by "flat" names rather than "sharp" names. So I've used the Roman numeral names indicating the bIII, bV, and bVII notes, rather than using the #II, #IV, and #VI names. Verbally, blues musicians call these the "flatted third," "flatted fifth," and "flatted seventh" notes.

The Blues Scale "Formula"

The blues scale uses the notes I, IIIb, IV, Vb, V, and VIIb, then ends on the I again. The blues scale leaves out the chromatic scale notes I# or IIb, II, III, VI, and VII. Here are the general note names of the notes of the blues scale, written out in solmi and Roman numeral names.

DO	ri	FA	fi	So	li	DO
I	bIII	IV	bV	V	bVII	I

And here's the "blues scale formula" followed by examples of three commonly used blues scales, in the keys of C, E, and Bb:

I	+	bIII	+	IV	+	bV	+	V	+	bVII	+	I
C		Eb		F		Gb		G		Bb		C
E		G		A		Bb		B		D		E
Bb		Db		Eb		E		F		Ab		Bb

The Incredible Importance of Scales

It's difficult to overestimate the importance of scales in making music. Although practicing scales alone can be boring, knowing that virtually all blues and rock riffs and solos lie hidden within the blues scale — just waiting for you to uncover them — is tremendously exciting! For many of the tens of thousands who have taken harmonica workshops with me, learning the blues scale on the "blues harp" has been almost a spiritual experience!

And for lovers of Country & Western music, understanding the "pentatonic scale" which lies beneath nearly all C & W riffs and solos — On harmonica, guitar, keyboard or fiddle — is an equally empowering experience!

The Pentatonic (C & W) Scale

The five note pentatonic scale is also derived from the chromatic scale. One pentatonic scale can begin on each of the chromatic scale's twelve notes. It is often used in rock music, and is especially important in creating improvisations in country or country & western music. There are more than one pentatonic scales, but this is the most commonly used one. Here it is in roman and solmi notation.

Do	RE	ME	SO	LA	DO
I	II	III	V	VI	I

And here is the "pentatonic scale formula" followed by three examples of pentatonic scales, in the often-used country & western keys of C, G, and E.

I +	II +	III +	V +	VI +	I
C	D	E	G	A	C
G	A	B	D	E	G
E	F#	G#	B	C#	E

Comparing Scales: Roman Names

Below, I've lined up all of the above scales so that you can see the way they compare to each other in roman numeral notation. Chromatic is first, then major, minor, blues, and pentatonic. Note the notes these scales have in common, and which are different.

C:	I	bII	II	bIII	III	IV	bV	V	bVI	VI	bVII	VII	I
M:	I		II		III	IV		V		VI		VII	I
m:	I		II	bIII		IV		V	bVI		bVII		I
B:	I			bIII		IV	bV	V			bVII		I
P:	I		II		III			V		VI			I

Comparing Scales: In the Key of C

Here are all the scales we've explored, lined up, using specific letter names, and all in the key of C — That is, beginning on the note named C. Again, the chromatic scale is the first line, then the major, minor, blues, and pentatonic scales.

C	Db	D	Eb	E	F	Gb	G	Ab	A	Bb	B	C
C		D		E	F		G		A		B	C
C		D	Eb		F		G	Ab		Bb		C
C			Eb		F	Gb	G			Bb		C
C		D		E			G		A			C

Scales on the NoteFinder™

The NoteFinder™ will help you to write any scale in any key. Simply place the roman numeral I on the small circle directly under the big circle note you wish to begin your scale on. If you put the I under the F, for instance, you can write any scale in the key of F.

Need an F blues scale? Look at the roman numeral notes used in the blues scale formula (written on the NoteFinder™): I - bIII - IV - bV - V - bVII - I).

Once the I note on the inner circle is lined up under the F note on the outer circle, you can see by the arrows that the bIII of this F scale is an Ab/G#, the IV is a A#/Bb, the bV is a B, the V is a C, the bVII is an D#/Eb, and the scale ends as it began on I and F.

Key of F Blues Scale

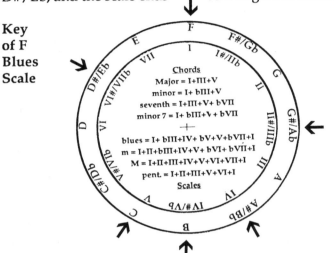

Want to find the notes of an Eb minor scale? Simply place the I of the inner circle under the note D#/Eb on the outer circle. Then read off the letter names of the notes (using flat names) that're above the roman numeral names of notes used in a minor scale: I - II - bIII - IV - V - bVI - bVII - I. Thus your Eb minor scale uses the notes Eb - F - Gb - Ab - Bb - B - Db - Eb.

Key of Eb Minor Scale

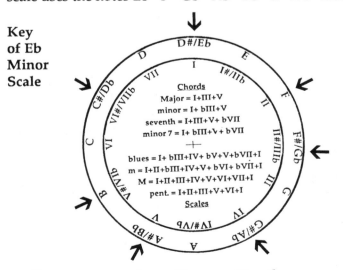

For your convenience, I have written the roman numeral "formulas" for the most important scales (and chords) on the inner circle of your NoteFinder™.

Scale Practice

Practice writing down the notes of a variety of scales in different keys, and play them on your instrument. A serious, versatile, musician should eventually be able to play a major scale, minor scale, blues scale, and pentatonic scale in each of the twelve possible keys — that is, able to play these scales beginning on each note of the chromatic scale.

What to Do With Scales

Now that we know how to play all these scales, the next logical question is: What do we *do* with them? And the answer is quite simple. As I said in my "musical alphabet" analogy, scales provide us with the basic building blocks of music.

There are two main ways to use these building blocks. They are used to create the tune, or **"melody"**, of a song. As I've said, the scale that is used to create a melody will have a very powerful effect on the feel of that melody. Use of a minor scale will produce a mournful melody, and use of a major scale will produce a bouncier, more cheerful melody. Use of a blues scale will produce, well, a bluesy melody!

We can also use scales for improvising. When we **"improvise"**, we create music as we play it. I think that improvisation is one of the most creative and satisfying ways of making music!

To improvise blues music, we use various combinations of notes chosen from the blues scale, which we play using a blues rhythm (described in the "Rhythm Section"). To improvise Country and Western music, we use notes from the pentatonic scale, and a country style rhythm. To improvise rock music, we use blues scale notes, or possibly pentatonic scale notes, and a rock rhythm. It's as simple as that, although you can spend a lifetime at it!

I will cover both of these topics, melody and improvisation, after discussing chords and chord structures. So just practice playing some scales now, and go on to the following sections on chords.

Scales can be used to create the tune, or melody of a song. They can also be used to **"improvise,"** that is, to create music spontaneously — to create your own music *while* you are playing it.

What Are Chords?

When playing scales, we only play one note at a time. Yet many notes sound good when played at the same time — and that's the definition of a "chord": **notes that sound good when played simultaneously.**

Four Common Types of Chords

There are many different types of chords, but luckily for us only four of them are commonly used in most music: **major, minor, seventh,** and **minor seventh chords.** Most chords are made up of either three or four notes, although certain jazz chords can use as many as seven notes at once.

Major chords are based on certain notes chosen from the major scale, and minor chords are based on certain notes chosen from the minor scale. Seventh and minor seventh chords are just regular major and minor chords with one extra note. It's pretty easy to figure out which notes are used to make up a chord, especially if you know how to use the roman numeral note names. I'll give you "formulas" to do this, just as I did for the various scales.

The Major Chord "Formula"

Since major chords are based on the major scale, they share that scale's brassy, bouncy, cheerful feel. A major chord is always made up of the first note, the third note, and the fifth note of the major scale. So if you already know the notes of a particular major scale, it's easy to create a major chord from that scale — Just locate the first, third and fifth notes of the C major scale. I have written out the C major scale and under-lined these notes, so you can see that a C major chord uses the notes C, E, and G.

C D E F G A B C

These same notes happen to be the I, the III, and the V note of the chromatic scale. So in roman numeral terms, a major chord looks like this, which we'll call the **"formula"** for creating a major chord:

Major Chord = I + III + V notes

Now create a major chord by looking at the notes of the chromatic scale. Choose the key (like D, which is usually written using #'s, page 30) of your major chord-to-be, and make that the first note of a chromatic scale. Then find the I, the III, and the V notes of that chromatic scale, and you've got your major chord!

I	I#	II	II#	III	IV	IV#	V	V#	VI	VI#	VII	I
D	D#	E	F	F#	G	G#	A	A#	B	C	C#	D

Even more simply, you can use your NoteFinder™ to locate the notes of a C major chord. Just place the I of the inner circle under the C note, and read off the notes above the III and the V, to get your C, E, and G.

Need a D# (D sharp) major chord? Line up the I of the inner circle under D#/Eb. Read the note above the III (which is G) and the note above the V (which is A#/Bb, but call it A#) to get the D# - G - A# notes of the D# major chord.

**D #
Major
Chord**

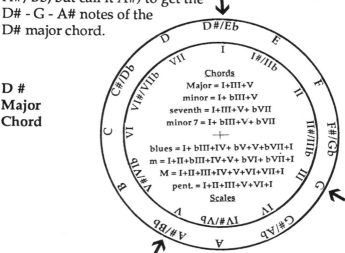

Pronouncing Major Chord Names

A major chord is always pronounced as "C major," or "B flat major", or "F sharp major", just as I've written them here. However, when musicians *write* major chords, we often use some shortcuts.

For instance, instead of writing out C major, we may just write out C M (C with a capital M) — or even just C (capital C). Instead of writing out Bb major, we can write Bb M or even just Bb. So if you see a single capital letter like G, or a single letter with a capital M, like GM, the writer is referring to a major chord.

The Minor Chord "Formula"

Since minor chords are based on the minor scale, they share that scale's poignant, wistful feel. A minor chord is always made up of the first, third, and fifth note of the minor scale. These are the I, the #II or bIII, and the V of the chromatic scale. In roman numeral terms, a minor chord looks like this:

Minor Chord = I + bIII + V notes

Use these roman numerals I, bIII, and V to find the notes of any minor chord. The easiest way to do this is with your NoteFinder™. Decide what key you want your minor chord to be in: Ab, for example. This will be the first note of your chord. To locate the other notes of your Ab minor chord, line up the I of the inner circle under the G#/Ab. Then add the note above the #II/bIII (which is a B), and the note above the V (which is an Eb). And this gives you the notes Ab, B, and Eb which make up a Ab minor chord.

Another Way to Find Minor Chords

If you already know the notes of a major chord, you can convert it to a minor chord just by lowering the middle note of the major chord by one chromatic note. This works because **the I and V note of a minor chord in any key are the same as the I and V notes of the major chord in that same key!** Take the C - E - G of the C major chord, lower the middle note from E to Eb, and presto, you have a C minor chord C - Eb - G!

Pronouncing Minor Chord Names

Minor chords are always pronounced "D minor" or "E flat minor", or "F sharp minor", just as I've written them here. However, when musicians write minor chords, we often use some shortcuts.

For instance, instead of writing out D minor, we may just write out D m (D with a lower case m), or even just a lower case d. So whenever you see a single letter followed by a lower case m, or a single lower case letter, the writer is referring to a minor chord.

The Seventh Chord "Formula"

"Seventh Chords" are **four note** chords. Their first three notes are exactly the same as the first three notes of the major chord, and are thus based on the major scale. But they also include a fourth note which is included in both the minor and blues scale. They have a more "tense" feeling than a major chord, but not as sad a feeling as a minor chord.

We might think of seventh chords as **"blues chords"**, since seventh chords are very often used in blues, as well as in rock and jazz music. The formula for a seventh chord is the same as the formula for a major chord, but adds a flat seventh (bVII) note.

Seventh Chord = I + III + V + bVII

Here is what your NoteFinder™ would look like if you were finding the notes of a G Seventh chord:

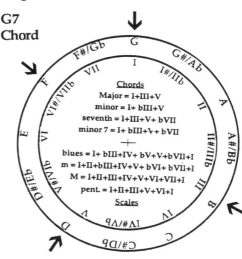

Don't let a slight mis-alignment of notes (like the III and the B in the key of G) throw you off! Just look for the note *nearest* the correct roman numeral.

Pronouncing Seventh Chord Names

A seventh chord is always pronounced as "D seventh," or "E flat seventh", or "F sharp seventh", just as I've written them here. When writing these chords down, we would notate them as "D7", "Eb7" or "F#7."

The Minor Seventh "Formula"

The last chord that we'll consider for now is the minor seventh chord, which is simply made up of the three notes of a regular minor chord, plus the same flatted seventh (bVII or #VI) note used in the "regular" seventh chord. Minor sevenths are most often used in playing jazz. Here's the formula for a minor seventh chord (I'll just use the b name):

Minor Seventh Chord = I + bIII + V + bVII

As you did with major, minor, and seventh chords, you can use the NoteFinder™ to locate the notes of any minor seventh chord, once you decide what key you want your minor seventh chord to be in.

Chord Practice

Now is a good time to practice writing down and playing a variety of major, minor, seventh, and minor seventh chords. You will be needing some of each when we get to the Chord Structure section that follows. If you can at least play C major, C minor, F major, F minor, and G seventh chords, you'll be in good shape!

C major:	C	E	G		C minor:	C	Eb	G
F major:	F	A	C		F minor:	F	Ab	C

G seventh: G B D F

If you are a vocalist, or play an instrument built to produce one note at a time, you may wish to practice playing the notes of a chord one after the other (since you can't play them simultaneously). This is called "arpeggiating" a chord (pronounced "are - pedge' - ee - ate - ing" with the accent on the second syllable).

One Last Chord Point: Inversions

Chords are often played with their notes in order, from low to high. This is called the **"root position"** of the chord. Most sheet music and chord charts leave the "position" of a chord up to the player. However, you may occasionally run into a situation in which the leader of a jamm session has specific ideas about what order in which to play the notes of a chord. Or, even more importantly, you may enjoy re-arranging the notes of a chord that you usually play in root position — it will sound excitingly different.

If the second note of the chord is played first (and the first note played last and highest), the chord is said to be in its **"first inversion."** If the third note of the chord is played first, the chord is said to be in its **"second inversion."** If a chord has four notes, and the fourth note is played first, the chord is said to be in its **"third inversion."**

For example, the root position of a C seventh chord (with its notes C, E, G, and Bb) is C - E - G - Bb. The first inversion would be E - G - Bb - C (first note now played last). The second inversion would be G - Bb - C - E, and the third inversion Bb - C - E - G.

root version of chord:	C	E	G	Bb	
first inversion:	E	G	Bb	C	
second inversion:	G	Bb	C	E
third inversion:	Bb	C	E	G

Chord Structures

Chords sound pleasant when they are played alone. But the real value of chords lies in giving us a **"chord structure"** to play, or to play along with.

Just as notes are played together to form chords, chords are played together to form chord structures. A chord structure is a series of chords, played one after the other, in a particular order, that sound good together. Each chord in a chord structure will be played for a particular number of beats.

And just as different types of chords, like major and minor chords, have different "feels" — different types of chord structures have different feels, and are used in playing different types of music. A blues chord structure helps to give a blues song its bluesy feel, just as the C & W chord structure helps to give a C & W song that country feel!

In a way, a chord structure is somewhat like a skeleton. A skeleton is a bony structure that supports the muscle, fat, and skin which "flesh out" every person, and make them look different. Yet all human skeletons are the same, with the same 206 bones attached to each other in the same ways.

The "skeleton" of a particular chord structure can be "fleshed out" musically with notes chosen from the appropriate scale. Sometimes this fleshing out is in the form of a memorized melody, or sometimes in the form of an instantly created improvisation.

We could also say that a chord structure is like the steel beam frame of an unfinished building. The carpenters, bricklayers, and painters can finish the same frame off in a variety of ways, and a musician can "finish" a chord structure, by adding the scale notes that make it sound like a completed piece of music.

Of course some musicians, especially keyboard and guitar players, can both provide a structure and flesh it out simultaneously. Others, especially those whose instruments can sound only one note at a time (like flutists, or vocalists), can either play the structure, or play along with it — but can't do both at once.

In the following sections, we will study the types of chord structures that are used in folk, rock, blues, and country music. Later on, we will study the scales that are used to improvise and play melodies along with these chord structures.

One Chord Structures

The simplest possible chord structure consists of just one chord, repeated over and over. This can get pretty boring when done by itself. If interesting lyrics or melodies or improvisations are played along with the single chord, even one chord structures can be quite musical.

In blues music, a single chord pattern (usually a seventh chord) against which lyrics and blues scale notes are played is called a **"boogie."** Please don't confuse this with a **"boogie woogie,"** which is one particular way of fleshing out the "twelve bar blues chord structure" that we will cover later in detail.

Blues artist John Lee Hooker often uses the one chord boogie structure in his work, and perhaps the most popular one chord boogie song ever was Canned Heat's late 1960's hit, *On The Road Again*.

For a more classical example, *Frere Jacques* can be considered a one chord song. How can we tell that? Because the notes of the melody can be played, or the lyrics can be sung, along with just one (major) chord. Rap music also sometimes uses a one chord structure against which lyrics are sung. However, one chord structures are generally considered somewhat limiting and repetitious.

Try playing a single chord over and over, like a C major, or a C seventh. Record a minute of each. Then play notes from the C major scale along with the C major chord recording, and the notes of the C blues scale along with the C seventh chord recording. This will be good practice for some of the exercises that I'll present later on.

Other Names for Chord Structures

Chord structures are sometimes known as **"chord changes"** (because, unless it is a one chord structure, the chord does change) or **"chord progressions."** In fact, sometimes these terms are shortened simply to **"changes"** or **"progression,"** as in "Let's play a blues progression in C."

When we increase the number of chords in a chord structure to two, we can really make some music. In fact, just playing a two chord structure energetically, without any melody or improvised scale notes, can sound good. But when we have more complex types of chord structures, we need convenient ways to describe them. Fortunately, such a way already exists, as the following section will demonstrate!

Roman Numeral Chord Names

Our old friends, the roman numeral names, can be used to refer to chords, just as we used them to refer to notes. Let's talk, for instance, about a I (one) chord and a V (five) chord. We know that these two chords have the same relationship between them as a I note and a V note. A I chord will always begin with the I note, and a V chord with the V note. (Even when we discuss inverted chords, we still use their I note for their name, and say, "Play a C7 chord in its first inversion: E - G - Bb - C.").

If we decide that our I chord should be a C chord, we automatically know (perhaps after a look at our NoteFinder™) that our V chord is a G chord. If we decide that our I chord should be an A# chord, then our V chord will automatically be an F chord.

Roman numeral names can be used to refer to any type of chord. If a chord just has a "plain" roman numeral name, like I, or IV, or VII (one, four, or seven chord), we can assume that it is a major chord. If it has a little "m" after it, like Im (one minor chord) or VIm (six minor chord), it is a minor chord. Minor chords are also sometimes indicated by lower case roman numerals, so that Im might also be written as i, and VIm as vi. If a chord is a seventh, it will (Surprise!) have a "7" written after its roman numeral, as in VII7 or IIIm7 (three minor seventh chord). Can you read these chord names?

IIm   V7   vii7   IVm   III   bII7

How can we tell whether the Roman numeral names are refering to single notes or chords? Well, for one thing, single notes won't have 'm' or '7' after them. But sometimes you have to just guess from the context — the same way you would tell whether 'I' means a 'DO' note, or whether David Harp is just talking about himself again!

Latin Chord Names

We can also, but less commonly, use the latin names for the I, IV, and V chords. A I chord could be called a **"tonic major chord,"** for instance. A IVm chord could be called a **"subdominant minor chord."** A V7 is quite often called a **"dominant seventh chord."** These latin names are well worth knowing!

The "Purpose" of Chord Structures

To put it very simply, the "purpose" of a chord progression is to begin with the I chord, then leave the I chord to build up a feeling of tension, then eventually return, or **"resolve,"** to the I chord (sometimes after more than a single verse). IV chords and V or V7 chords, or other chords that can be substituted for them, are what we use to make this journey away from, and then back to, the I chord. Even the most complex jazz can be described or analyzed as making this trip: Starting on the I chord, then going away, then resolving back to the I chord.

About Bars and Measures

In a later section we will consider the different rhythms used when playing various styles of music. But there's one aspect of musical timing that you must know in order to be able to play chord structures.

As you unconsciously understand when you tap your foot along to a piece of music, almost all of our culture's music is played along with a steady pulse, known as the **"beat."** Music is also divided into slightly larger rhythmic chunks, known either as **"bars"** or **"measures."** Most bars or measures are either three or four beats long.

Reading Chord Charts

We can describe a chord structure in writing by simply listing the chords in it. We might say, for example, that most two chord folk structures are I and V chord structures. Of course, I and V is a very general name for the structure — it merely tells us the relationship between the two chords that are used in the structure. Fortunately for people who want to be able to play together without much preparation, there is a much more specific way of writing chord structures down.

"Chord Charts" are used to tell musicians which chords are used in the structure of a song. In a chord chart, each time the chord appears, it represents one bar or measure of that chord. The chords are usually separated by a dash. So this chord chart represents two bars of a I chord, then two bars of a V chord.

I - I - V - V (for a total of four bars)

This simple I - I - V - V chord chart represents one **"verse"** of a chord structure that is four bars long. Just as in any song, one verse of a chord structure is repeated over and over, for the length of the song or piece. Most songs are at least three verses long — that is, the chord structure is repeated three or more times.

When reading chord charts like the I - I - V - V, we can refer to measure or bar numbers, and say things like "It changes to the five chord for the third bar."

Two Chord Folk Songs, and Charts

Two chord folk music structures are usually composed of a I chord and a V7 chord, or, in other words, a major chord based on the I note and a seventh chord based on a V note. These are called I - V ("one five") chord structures. The latin names of these chords are the "tonic major" and "dominant seventh."

If a single measure is split between two chords, the two chords in one measure are separated by a **"slash mark"** instead of a dash, like I/V7. **I/V7**

Look at the chord structure for one verse of the two chord folk song, *Skip To My Lou*. Each slash mark above the lyrics represents one beat, that is, one tap of your foot. You can see that each chord is played for four beats, or one bar, except for the last two chords, which are played for two beats each. The chord changes are written out below each line:

```
\   \   \         \   \   \   \           \
Lou Lou skip to my Lou  Lou Lou skip to my Lou
I                       V7
\   \   \         \   \         \     \   \
Lou Lou skip to my Lou  Skip to my Lou my dar- lin'
I                       V7               I
```

Skip to My Lou could also be written out as follows. Notice the slash in the last bar, telling us that each chord gets only two beats (half of the last bar):

I - V7 - I - V7/I

Finding Specific Chords for Songs

Of course, a chord chart written out using roman numeral names only tells you the relationship between the chords. You must then decide which of the twelve chromatic scale notes to base your I chord on.

Once you've chosen the specific letter name of the I chord, you can use The NoteFinder™ to locate the V chord that goes with it. To play *Skip To My Lou* in the key of C, we would let C be the I chord, and use The NoteFinder™ to find out that the V chord in the key of C is a G chord. The chord chart would then look like this:

C - G7 - C - G7/C   instead of   I - V7 - I - V7/I

Another Two Chord Folk Structure

Here's another very popular two chord folk structure. Each verse begins with three four beat measures of I chord, then four measures of V7 chord, then ends with one measure of I chord. So one 32 beat verse of this chord structure looks like this:

I - I - I - V7 - V7 - V7 - V7 - I (for a total of 8 bars)

This is the chord structure for folk songs like *Ain't Gonna Rain No More*, Hank Williams' *Jambalaya*, *Tom Dooley*, *Irene Goodnight*, and many more.

Chord Charts Using Letter Names

Sometimes chord charts are more specific, and are already written out for you using letter names of chords. Just as with the roman numerals, each letter name (separated by a dash) represents one bar or measure of a chord, and if a bar needs to be divided between two chords, they will be separated by a slash mark.

For instance, in the key of C, the specific chords needed to play one verse of the very popular two chord folk structure, above, would be these (check it on the NoteFinder™):

C - C - C - G7 - G7 - G7 - G7 - C

To play it in the key of E, you would use :

E - E - E - B7 - B7 - B7 - B7 - E

Two Chord Rock and Roll Songs

Many rock and roll songs are also based on a two chord structure, although a rock two chord structure is likely to be made up of the I and the IV7 (IV seventh or subdominant seventh) chords. The J. Geils band 1970 hit, *Wait*, as well as Question Mark and the Mysterians' 1965 hit, *96 Tears*, are both based on this simple I - IV7 structure.

It is composed of just a single four beat bar of I chord followed by a bar of IV7, repeated over and over with lyrics and scale notes added. In the key of C, its chords would be C - F7, and in the key of Bb, its chords would be Bb - Eb7 (as The NoteFinder™ will show you).

I - IV7   C - F7   Bb - Eb7

Simply playing these chords for four beats each on a guitar or keyboard won't sound very exciting. However, if you can add some rock and roll rhythm (coming up soon!) to the chords, you'll have feet tapping in no time!

More On Reading Chord Charts

Chord charts come in many different forms. They can be as simple as the chords written out just like the ones above, scrawled on scraps of paper during a jamm session. Or they may come written above a five line staff, with timing slashes, the lyrics, and even the melody of the song written beneath them. Often the bars of a song are divided by bar lines, which are just vertical lines between measures.

Two New Chord Chart Symbols

Two symbols are very commonly used when writing chord charts, especially if the writer is in a hurry, or short on space to write in. A diagonal line, with a dot on each side, means that we must repeat the previous bar. If there are two of these in a row, we repeat the previous chord two more times, for a total of three.

A symbol composed of two vertical lines, with two dots to the left of the lines, tells us to repeat the entire piece. If I wanted, I could put a repeat sign after every chord structure, to tell you to play them over and over again.

Here's a new way of writing out the popular two chord folk structure: I - I - I - V7 - V7 - V7 - V7 - I. It's hand-written as a chord chart on a staff with timing slashes, bar repeat signs, and a repeat verse sign.

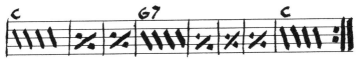

First and Second Endings

Chord charts sometimes also include **"first end-ings"** and **"second endings."** These symbols are an easy way to indicate that the first time we play a verse of the chord structure, we end it one way, and the second time we play a verse, we end it differently.

This eight bar I - V chord structure below has a repeat sign at the end, as well as two extra bars written under a second ending symbol. So we know that after playing one verse, we must repeat it. But when playing the first verse, we end with two bars of V chord, as they're the chords under the first ending symbol. When we play the second verse, we change it to end on one bar of V, and a final bar of I, since they are the chords under the second ending symbol.

$$\boxed{1.} \qquad \boxed{2.}$$
I - I - V - V - I - I - V - V :|| V - I

This second ending gives the chord structure a more "finished" feel, rather than leading the listener to expect yet another verse. This is because chord progressions "want" to end on the I chord (page 43).

The Rhythm Section

"**Rhythm**" might be defined as the way in which the basic pulse, or **"beat,"** of a piece of music is broken up into smaller pieces. Certain rhythms are characteristic of certain styles of music. After learning to play different rhythms, you can then apply them to the appropriate chord structures for those styles of music.

The following rhythms are meant to give you some ideas on the ways in which rhythms can be applied to chord structures. For a more complete study of rhythm, please see the description of my *Instant Rhythm Kit* method on page 78, and listen to lots of music in the styles that you want to play in.

A Classic Rock "Backbeat" Rhythm

Most rock and roll is broken into four beat measures or bars. You can simply tap your foot steadily, and count "one two three four." It won't sound wrong, but it won't sound very rocking either.

You can convert that simple "one two three four" into a typical rock and roll **"backbeat"** rhythm by doing two things. First, break each beat into two parts: "one and two and three and four and." Once that feels comfortable, emphasize the beats occuring on the count of "two" and "four" by tapping your foot louder on them, or saying them louder. Once again, I'll use a slash mark to represent the exact time that your foot should hit the floor, if you're tapping.

    \\   \\   \\   \\

"one and **two** and three and **four** and"

Simply playing the two chord rock and roll structure using two chords and this rhythm will sound great!

A Classic Country Rhythm

Like rock, much country music is broken up into four beat measures. However, the classic country rhythm differs from the classic rock rhythm in subtle but important ways. It tends to break the second and fourth beats only into two parts, and all notes are emphasized equally, with the first note of each measure slightly louder.

    \\   \\   \\   \\

"one   two and three   four and"

If you want to play a country rhythm with a rock and roll feeling, try emphasizing each second and fourth beat, for a country-rock rhythm.

    \\   \\   \\   \\

"one   **two** and three   **four** and"

A Classic Blues "Shuffle" Rhythm

To play either blues or jazz music, it is necessary to learn to **"swing"** the beat. When you just broke the country and rock beats into two parts, each of the two parts (the "one" and the "and," for example) were roughly equal in length. But swinging the beat means that when you break a single blues or jazz beat into two parts, the first should be longer than the second. The first part should be emphasized slightly, as well. I might write this out as:

\   \   \   \
"onne 'a **twoo** 'a **threee** 'a **foour** 'a"

Many blues players describe this as letting the first part ("one") of the beat take up three-quarters of the beat, and letting the second part (" 'a ") of the beat take up one-quarter of the beat. This is often called a **"shuffle"** beat, or a **"boogie-woogie"** beat.

Other blues players prefer to use "triplet" timing, as described in the jazz section below.

A Classic Jazz Rhythm

Jazz players also swing the beat, but most jazz musicians tend to think of letting the first part ("one") of the beat take up two-thirds of the beat, and letting the second part (" 'an ") take up one-third of the beat. This is usually called **"triplet"** timing, or a "triplet beat." It isn't quite as extreme an emphasis on the first part of each beat as in shuffle timing.

\   \   \   \
"one 'an **two** 'an **three** 'an **four** 'an"

This rhythm can also be interpreted like this, with the "and" taking two-thirds of a beat, and the "a" taking one third.

\   \   \   \
"one   and a   **two**   and a"

Or even like this, which sounds exactly like the rhythm just above, but has half as many beats.

\   \
"one   and a   **two**   and a

\   \
three   and a   **four**   and a"

Of course, you will only get the feel of blues and jazz rhythm by listening to lots of it, so you've got your work cut out for you!

A Word to the Rhythmically Insecure

If these rhythms seem unfamiliar or difficult to you, check out my *Instant Rhythm Kit* offer on page 78.

More Chord Structures

Thousands of chord structures exist. So I'm not going to cover them all. But now that you understand two chord structures, I would like to describe some of my favorite three chord structures. Knowing these three chord structures will enable you to play many thousands of songs, as some of our culture's finest blues, folk, rock, and pop songs use only three chords.

Just about all three chord structures use the I, the IV, and the V chords in one form or another. Make sure you know the latin names of these three crucial chords as well: the **tonic chord** (which is the I chord), the **dominant chord** (the IV), and the **dominant chord** (the V).

These three chords are so important that it wouldn't be a bad idea to learn the I, IV, and V of every key. The letters names in the top row of this chart represent both the key and the I note, the middle row has the IV notes, and the bottom row the V notes, all with sharp names. So in C, the I - IV - V is C - F - G.

I:	C	C#	D	D#	E	F	F#	G	G#	A	A#	B
IV:	F	F#	G	G#	A	A#	B	C	C#	D	D#	E
V:	G	G#	A	A#	B	C	C#	D	D#	E	F	F#

A Hint for Flautists and Singers

Practice playing these chord structures using arpeggiated chords, that is, playing each note of the chord separately. Use your NoteFinder™, if necessary, to determine the notes of a chord, then play each note for one beat. If you are playing a three note chord that must last for four beats, feel free to repeat any of the chord notes twice. For instance, to make a C major chord C - E - G fit into four beats, try playing C - E - G - E for one beat each, or end up on the next highest C by playing C - E - G - C.

Singers, you may need the use of another instrument to really understand these chord structures. Choose a comfortable key to sing in. Have an instrumentalist friend play (and record) some of the following chord structure verses using the regular chords, and then some verses using the arpeggiated notes of the chords.

Then begin by singing along with the arpeggiations that your friend plays. When that feels comfortable, sing the arpeggiated notes along with the regular (not arpeggiated) chord structure. It may sound like a lot of work, but it will increase both your understanding of music theory and your singing abilities considerably! If you don't have a friend with a guitar or piano, you may want to obtain the cassette that demonstrates the music in this book.

The Twelve Bar Blues Structure

This may be the single most popular chord structure in the history of the world. It's used in most blues music, in a lot of rock, and in quite a bit of jazz. Elvis, the Beatles, the Stones, the Batman theme — the twelve bar blues shows up everywhere. It's probably also the most used chord structure for improvising.

A bar or measure is a way of breaking up a song into smaller numbers of beats. Most blues songs use a four beat bar. A twelve bar blues means each verse of chord structure is twelve bars (12 x 4 = 48 beats) long.

Below you will find chord charts for the simplest possible twelve bar blues progression in roman numeral notation, followed by chord charts for "blues changes" in the keys of C and Eb, for examples of specific keys. Literally thousands of variations on this structure exist, and we will consider some in the jazz section later on. But learn this one, and you'll be able to make lots of music with players the world over. Use your NoteFinder™ to create twelve bar blues in any key, and play a few, using a blues shuffle rhythm!

I - I - I - I - IV - IV - I - I - V7 - IV - I - I

C - C - C - C - F - F - C - C - G7 - F - C - C

Eb - Eb - Eb - Eb - Ab - Ab- Eb - Eb - Bb7 - Ab - Eb - Eb

Blues Structure Chord Charts

Here's what a handwritten chord chart for a twelve bar blues in the key of E might look like. I have used bar repeat marks and a final repeat symbol, which tells you to play the whole thing again. You're apt to see something like this at a jamm session. And it's good to be able to know how to write one out yourself, if necessary!

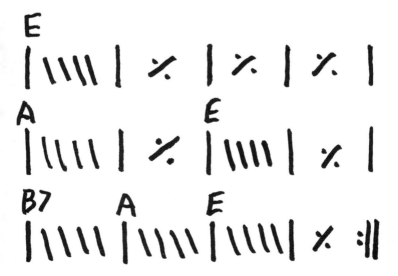

Describing a Twelve Bar in Words

When describing a twelve bar blues, musicians often refer to the parts of it as the **"first tonic"** part (meaning bars 1 to 4), **"first subdominant"** (bars 5 and 6), **"second tonic"** (bars 7 and 8), **"dominant"** (bar 9), **"second subdominant"** (bar 10), and **"third tonic"** (bars 11 and 12), which includes a **"turnaround,"** (which I'll describe in the next section).

1 st tonic   1 st sub   2nd ton   dom   2nd sub   3rd ton

I - I - I - I -   IV - IV   - I - I -   V7   - IV   - I - I

"Turnarounds"

Often, the last two, three, or four beats of a standard blues progression verse return to the V7 chord, to help show that one verse is ending, and another about to begin. This is helpful, because when a verse ends on the I chord, and another begins on the I chord, it might not be clear just where one verse ends and the next begins. (Yelling out "This verse is over!" is considered crude.) We call this brief return to the V7 a **"turnaround."** Following is a blues progression with a four beat turnaround — That is, four beats of V7.

I - I - I - I - IV - IV - I - I - V7 - IV - I - V7
                                                   turnaround

An equally good turnaround could feature two beats of V7 at the end of the third tonic part, like this:

I - I - I - I - IV - IV - I - I - V7 - IV - I - I/V7
                                                    turnaround

---

Remember: One bar or measure (represented by a single chord symbol separated by a dash) is held for four beats. When two chord symbols are separated by a slash, each chord is held for two beats.

Chord Substitutions in the Blues

"Chord substitution" simply means that we substitute one chord for another in a chord structure. We substitute chords to make a chord structure more complex, and thus more "interesting sounding." It is a very important technique for playing jazz, although somewhat less crucial for blues players.

For example, if we like, we can substitute a IV7 chord for any of the IV chords in a blues progression. This will give the song a somewhat more tense feel. We can also substitute a I7 chord for some of the I chords, although usually not for all of them — it's most common to use a single bar of I7 chord at the end of the tonic parts. Here's a twelve bar blues with some I7 and IV7 substitutions, which I've underlined.

I - I - I - I7 - IV - IV7 - I - I7 - V7 - IV7 - I - V7

The Twelve Bar Rock Structure

When rock and roll utilizes the twelve bar structure, it often substitutes an extra bar of V7 chord in the place of the IV chord in the second subdominant, that is, in the tenth bar of the chord structure. Again, I've underlined the substitution.

Rock : I - I - I - I7 - IV - IV7 - I - I7 - V7 - <u>V7</u> - I7 - V7

Blues: I - I - I - I7 - IV - IV7 - I - I7 - V7 - IV - I7 - V7

And, naturally, another important difference between the Blues Twelve Bar and the Rock Twelve Bar is that the Rock Twelve Bar is played using a rock rhythm instead of a blues rhythm (page 47).

The Blues or Rock "Intro"

Before the actual first verse begins, a blues or rock song often begins with a two or four bar introduction, or **"intro."** This intro is usually the same as the last four or two bars of a regular twelve bar chord structure, tacked on in *front* of the first verse.

If you know the two most popular chord structures for rock and blues intros, you won't be so confused if a blues "doesn't quite seem to follow the standard twelve bar structure in the first verse." What's wrong with it? Nothing — it probably just starts off with an introduction!

If an intro is four bars long, it will most likely have a chord structure like V7 - IV - I - V7, or for example in the key of C, a G7 - F - C - G7 structure.

A two bar intro will probably have a chord structure similar to either I - I/V7, or I - V7. In the key of C, this would be C - C/G7, or C - G7.

Remember: The intro is played only once, at the very beginning of the song, and then you go straight to the regular chord structure. Here is a chord chart for a four bar intro and one complete verse of a twelve bar blues in the key of C.

G7 - F - C - G7

    C - C - C - C7 - F - F7 - C - C7 - G7 - F7 - C - G7

The Minor Twelve Bar Blues

A very satisfying, if mournful, variation on the twelve bar blues substitutes a minor chord for most of the I or IV major or seventh chords of the regular twelve bar blues (for some reason the V7 chord almost always remains the same, rather than changing to a minor V chord).

Minor blues are usually played very slowly, and often substitute one measure of iv (minor fourth) chord for the expected measure of i (minor first) chord in the second measure of the twelve bar (underlined). Here's the simplest possible minor twelve bar blues, written out in roman notation (notice my use of lower case roman numerals to represent minor chords), and in the key of E.

i - <u>iv</u> - i - i - iv - iv - i - i - V7 - iv - i - V7

Em - Am - Em - Em - Am - Am - Em - Em
B7 - Am - Em - B7

Minor Blues Turnarounds

Minor blues often tend to have more complex turnarounds than major blues, such as the eight beat i/iv - i/V7. It's composed, of course, of two beats of i chord, two beats of iv chord, two more beats of i chord, and two beats of V7 chord. Try it instead of the simpler I - V7 turnarounds that I've been using in the examples above. In C, it'd look like Cm/Fm - Cm/G7.

Here's a minor twelve bar blues with this fancier turnaround, written out in roman numeral notation and in the keys of C and then F. In the jazz section, I'll present some jazzier versions of the minor blues!

i - iv - i - i - iv - iv - i - i - V7 - iv - i/iv - i/V7

Cm - Fm - Cm - Cm - Fm - Fm - Cm - Cm
G7 - Fm - Cm/Fm - Cm/G7

Fm - Bbm - Fm - Fm - Bbm - Bbm - Fm - Fm
C7 - Bbm - Fm/Bbm - Fm/C7

Country & Western Structures

Like the blues, country and western music has a few standardized chord structures that are extremely popular. But instead of being twelve bars long, the three most common country chord structures are eight bars long, with four beats to the bar. Like the blues, they also use only the I, the IV, and the V chords, although for variety the V7 chord can be used in place of the V chord.

This standard C & W structure can be found in some of country's most famous songs, like Ed and Patsy Bruce's unforgettable *Mamas, Don't Let Your Babies Grow Up To Be Cowboys*. Here it is, in roman numerals and G.

I - IV - V7 - I - I - IV - V7 - I

G - C - D7 - G - G - C - D7 - G

Sometimes, instead of repeating the I - IV - V - I chords twice, as in the above eight bar, each of the chords is played twice. Bobby Emmons' and Chip Momar's *Luckenbach, Texas* uses this type of chord changes, presented in roman notation and key of E.

I - I - IV - IV - V - V - I - I

E - E - A - A - B - B - E - E

One more eight bar country chord structure is used in songs as diverse as *The Wreck of the Old 97* and the Rolling Stones' country rock classic *Honky Tonk Women*. Notice that the seventh measure is split between the I chord and the V chord.

If you like, feel free to use a V7 chord for any of the V chords, especially for the last (two beat) V chord, as I do here in my key of G version.

I - IV - I - V - I - IV - I/V - I

G - C - G - D - G - C - G/D7 - G

Folk Song Chord Structures

By far the majority of American folk songs use a three chord structure. Most begin on the I chord, end on either the I or the V chord, and include some IV chord (and maybe some V) somewhere in the middle.

Often, two different songs share the same chord structure, like *Oh When The Saints Go Marching In* and *Red River Valley*, whose chord structures both look like this (in roman numeral notation, and the key of D):

I - I - I - V - I - IV - I/V - I

D - D - D - A - D - G - D/A - D

About Verse and Chorus Structure

Although most songs use the same chord structure repeated over and over, some songs use what is often called a **"verse and chorus"** structure.

The **"chorus"** (which is a variation of the verse's chord structure) can confuse you, if you're not aware that it can exist. Stephen Foster's *Swanee River* demonstrates this well. Each **main verse** ("Way down upon the Swanee River...") has this chord structure (slightly simplified):

I/IV - I/IV - I - V7 - I/V7 - I/IV - I/V7 - I

Each **chorus** ("All the world is sad and dreary...") has this somewhat different chord structure. In a song book or chord chart a chorus will usually be marked with the word "chorus" or "cho."

V7 - I - IV - I/V7 - I/V7 - I/IV - I/V7 - I

So when writing out this chord structure, we would have to include both parts, perhaps like this:

Verse: I/IV - I/IV - I - V7 - I/V7 - I/IV - I/V7 - I

Cho: V7 - I - IV - I/V7 - I/V7 - I/IV - I/V7 - I

Pop Song Chord Structures

Many simpler pop songs have chord structures similar to folk songs, in that they use I, IV, and V chords exclusively. Often, a pop song will include a section that goes back and forth between the I and IV chords, then include a V chord before returning to end on the I chord. The Rolling Stones' *Satisfaction,* and *You Are My Sunshine* are good examples of this type of chord structure, although they differ from each other in how long each I and IV chord is held for. Here are two common pop style variations.

I - I - IV - I - IV - I - I/V - I

I - IV - I - IV - I/IV - I/IV - I/V - I

Bob Dylan Style Chord Structures

Bob Dylan often uses a similar chord structure, especially in his early songs, but in highly creative ways. In *Blowing In The Wind,* for example, he makes a I/IV - I - I/IV - V sequence a repeated part of his chord structure, using it three times before finishing it off with a different arrangement of I, IV, and V chords. And in his wonderful song *Hey Mr. Tambourine Man,* he begins on the IV chord instead of the I, giving the song its slightly eerie or other-worldly feel. Studying Mr. Dylan's early chord structures is a great way to learn creative usage of the I, IV, and V chords — buy a Dylan songbook, and get to it!

The 1950's Rock 'n Roll Structure

The rock and roll music of the 1950's and early 1960's, when not using the twelve bar blues structure or one of its variations, often featured the following four chord structure. *Duke of Earl* is one of the best-known examples of it.

The basic '50's rock structure verse uses a VIm chord, that is, a minor sixth chord (which we could also notate as vi). Here it is, in roman numeral and in the keys of C, G, and E.

I - VIm - IV - V7   G - Em - C - D7

C - Am - F - G7   E - C#m - A - B7

Use your NoteFinder™ to find the chords in any key. You should already be great at locating I, IV, and V chords. Now you just have to look at the letter name above the VI on the inner circle. Write it down as a minor chord, and you can be a *Teen Angel*, too!

Songs of this type may sometimes have a chorus, which generally uses the chords I, IV, and V, and often begins on the IV, then goes to the V, before ending on the I. But it is the main verse that is instantly recognizable, and very satisfying! And also very easy to play on many instruments, and included in both my *Instant Guitar* and *Blues & Rock Harmonica Made Easy* instructionals (page 78).

How to Play Any Type of Music

You now know how to use letter names and roman numerals to refer to notes and chords. You know the most important scales, the most common chord progressions, and the basic rhythms for many styles of music. And that's really all you need to know to play any type of music!

Yes, it's true. If you know the scale used to play a style of music, one or more of the common chord structures used, and the basic rhythm, you're in business!

How to Play the Blues

For example, let's say that you can play some folk tunes on the piano, but you've never played blues music before. Here's what you do.

1) Practice saying and tapping the blues shuffle rhythm from page 48.

2) Choose an easy key to play in, C for example. Guitar players may prefer the keys of E or A.

3) Write out your own chord chart for a twelve bar blues progression in the key of C (or E or A), using your NoteFinder™ if necessary.

4) Practice playing the chords of the progression, using the shuffle rhythm if possible, using your left hand only.

5) Learn the notes of the C blues scale, using the NoteFinder™ if you need to. Practice them using your right hand only, in the shuffle rhythm, if you can, if not, in some even simpler rhythm.

6) Now play the chords with your left hand, while you add some blues scale notes with your right.

Of course, it will be a little different for guitar players, who need to play both chords and scales with just one hand to strum and pick. And it will be very different for clarinetists, flutists, and other instrumentalists who can only play one note at a time. You single-noters, as I have said, will have to arpeggiate your chords when practicing the chord structures.

You may have the most fun when playing along with recorded music (like my cassette), or with other musicians who can provide solid chord structures for you to play along with. It's often easier to learn to concentrate on playing nice solos using blues scale notes with your right hand if you don't have to concentrate on providing your own chord structure with your left hand at the same exact time!

How to Play Country & Western

Want to spend an evening jamming C & W music with your friends when you visit Texas for the first time? Study your pentatonic scales and the C & W chord structures described in this book, and be ready to kick out the jamms! What if they want to play a song you've never heard of, with a different chord structure than the ones in here? Just ask 'em to write you out a chord chart, study it for a minute, and play!

When improvising C & W using the pentatonic scale, it is common to begin a sequence of notes on the V note *below* the scale, add the VI note, and then play the entire scale. Why? I'm not sure, but try playing these notes (below in roman and G notation) and you'll hear how right it sounds!

V - VI - I - II - III - V - VI - I

D - E - G - A - B - D - E - G

This stuff comes out great (and easily) on the harmonica. If you like the wailing C & W sound of Willie Nelson's harp player (Mickey Rafael), or of Nashville's incomparable Charlie McCoy, please read about my C & W Harmonica package on page 79.

How to Play Rock Music

If you want to rock, just practice playing the chords of the Two Chord Rock (page 45) or the Fifties Rock (page 55) or the Twelve Bar Rock (page 52) chord structures with the rock rhythm (page 47), and try using either the blues or pentatonic scale for fleshing out the structure. In rock, the bV note of the blues scale is less often used than it is in blues. And go to a music store to find a songbook by your favorite group — just make sure you get one with the chords clearly indicated.

How to Play Folk Music

Since most folk songs have simple chord structures, they are easy to play right away. Just get a songbook that has the chords to each song, and go for it!

Now that you understand the basic elements of music theory, you can play just about anything, even styles of music not covered in this book. All you need to do is to figure out what it is you need to know, and then learn it. Want to play Eastern European folk music, in the style of the Gypsy and Jewish cultures of that region? Just practice your minor scales, and get some chord charts for the songs that you want to learn.

The following sections on improvisation and composition will help to show you how to use the material that you already know — to play, improvise, and compose any type of music!

Improvisation and Melody

There are hundreds of musical cultures. There are thousands of different styles of playing music. But I believe that there are only two main ways of playing. One is to play music that other people (or ourselves) have already created, by reading it from notation or memorizing it. The other way is to improvise — that is, to spontaneously create music as we play it.

What Is Improvisation?

When we improvise, we are usually playing along with a chord structure that has already been agreed upon by the musicians. So the chords that we play are planned, but not the exact notes that we use to flesh out the chords.

We choose these "fleshing out" notes from the appropriate scale: When we play blues, we choose them from the blues scale, when we play C & W, we choose them from the pentatonic scale. The act of choosing the notes with which we flesh out the chord structure is the art of improvisation.

What Is Melody?

The musical term **"melody"** refers simply to a sequence of notes that has been created, and which can be repeated (from memory or notation). Another word for melody is **"tune."** Melody notes are usually chosen from within a particular scale, although notes that are not in the scale are occasionally used for variety. Melodies are not created spontaneously, while playing — and that's the difference between a melody and an improvisation.

Melody and improvisation are not completely separate. Some improvisors like to begin by playing a melody along with a chord structure, then more or less abandoning the melody and improvising along with the chord structure, then perhaps returning to the melody at the end of the song. And many improvised pieces have been recorded, and written down. When another artist plays them, note for note, they are then no longer an improvisation, but a melody. We will study melody a bit more when discussing song composition. Now it's time to talk improvisation!

Beginning Improvisation

There are hundreds of books about the art of improvisation. If you are serious about your music, you may want to buy and study a book that teaches improvisation exercises for your instrument, be it bassoon or xylophone. However, a few simple guidelines can get you improvising right away — and having lots of fun as well — especially if you have been mostly playing non-improvised music up until now.

As you know, improvising involves playing along with a chord structure. So make sure that you are really familiar with at least one of the chord structures in this book before beginning to improvise. And no matter what instrument you play, having some recorded chord structures in keys that are easy for you will be very helpful. So record them yourself as I've already explained, get a friend to record some for you, or use my cassette.

I will mostly be using the twelve bar blues structure to demonstrate the various improvisation strategies. Please review it now (in roman notation, and in the key of C) if you have any questions about it.

I - I - I - I - IV - IV - I - I - V7 - IV - I - V7

C - C - C - C - F - F - C - C - G7 - F - C - G7

The blues structure is not only the most commonly used improvisational structure — it's my favorite, too!

Tension and Relaxation

When improvising, we want to choose notes that sound interesting when played along with the chord structure that we are using. Some notes, especially the root (first note) of a chord, will sound very "right," or "relaxed," when played along with that same chord. Other notes will sound "tense," and yet others will sound just plain wrong, especially if held for long.

The balance between relaxation and tension is an art, and every improviser has his or her own preferred level of tension. I'll give you a chart, and discuss which notes are more relaxed, and which are more tense, in the following sections, but I can't tell you how many of each to play. After you spend some time playing, you'll know what feels right to you. If your improvisations are too relaxed, too predictable — they'll be boring. If they're too tense, too unpredictable — they'll sound wrong. What's in between? That's for you to discover, by doing it!

The Blues I Chord "Tension Chart"

What notes sound "rightest" will differ depending on what style of music you're playing — This chart is for blues only, and only covers notes in the blues scale, and the notes used in the I7 blues chord. You can see that the I, III, and V notes of the I major chord sound very right, very relaxed. The IV note is in the middle, and the bVII, bIII, and bV are "tenser." Other notes (like, for example, the bII or bVI during a I chord) sound so "wrong" in blues playing that we can scarcely use them at all (but see below). A warning: Different notes will also sound more or less tense during the IV and V chords of this same blues!

MoreRelaxed				More Tense		
I	III	V	IV	bVII	bIII	bV

Of course, putting in a tense note or two for just a second or fraction of a second can sound great, whereas if you held that same note for an entire measure, people would run screaming from the room! So don't linger too much on the "relaxed" notes, nor avoid the "tense" ones — the chart is for your information, only...

Using Chord Notes to Improvise

Perhaps the easiest way to improvise is to use the notes that make up the chords themselves during the chord structures. The simplest form of chordal improvisation involves just that — playing the arpeggiated notes of the chord along with the chord structure. In the standard blues progression, that requires knowing the notes of only three chords: the I7 chord, the IV7 chord, and the V7 chord.

Notes of the I, IV, and V Chords

When you use chord notes to improvise with in a blues progression, they will sound better if you use seventh chord arpeggiations instead of major chord arpeggiations, even if the chord progression itself uses major chords. So use the I7 chord during the I chord parts of the progression, and the IV7 chord during the IV chord parts. In the key of C, this would mean using the following notes during each chord:

I chords: C - E - G - Bb notes

IV chords: F - A - C - Eb notes

V chords: G - B - D - F notes

Since each measure or bar of the blues is four beats long, begin simply by playing each note of the chord for one beat. Use a four beat V7 turnaround, and fit your entire arpeggiated V7 chord into the turnaround.

Now try using different variations of these chord notes during each I, IV, and V part of the blues. For example, instead of just playing the C - E - G - Bb notes in order, fill two bars of the I chord by playing them first from low to high (as you did before), then back from high note to low.

C - E - G - Bb - Bb - G - E - C

Instead of playing them with one note per beat:
a) play some at two per beat, or
b) hold one that you like for two beats, play the next two for half a beat each, and play the last for one beat, or
c) play the first two for a beat each, the last two for a half a beat each, with one beat of silence.
Try these examples (slash marks show the beat, and a slash without a note under it is a beat of silence).

```
      \       \       \       \
a)    C   C   E   E   G   G   Bb  Bb

      \\      \       \              \    \    \          \
b)    C       E   G   Bb      c)    C    E    G    Bb
```

Insert a beat or part of a beat of silence anywhere to make the note that comes after more emphasized.

Practice playing the notes in a blues shuffle rhythm. Begin by playing one particular note twice per (broken up) beat. Then experiment with playing two *different* notes per beat, shuffle time (one note gets three-quarters of a beat, and the other one-quarter).

If this all seems intimidating at first, just choose two notes from each chord, and play combinations of only those two notes during that chord of the blues progression. If you make sure that you change to the correct chord at the correct time, even your two note improvisations will sound good. And of course, this same set of chord techniques described above can be used for improvising with any chord structure!

Using Scale Notes to Improvise

Although chord notes are very safe to use, in the sense that they will never sound wrong when played along with the appropriate chords of the chord progression — let's face it — they do not provide a great deal of excitement in improvisation. We can add lots of more interesting notes by using a *scale* to improvise with a progression. However, we also increase our chances of playing notes that sound wrong, if we don't choose those notes with some care.

If we play the appropriate scale, most of its notes will sound reasonably right, most of the time. For example, take the blues scale, probably the most popular improvising scale ever!

Blues Scale Improv

Choose a key to play in. It should be a key that you have already recorded some verses of the blues progression in (or one that is on the cassette). The key you have decided to play the blues chord structure in, will be the key of the blues scale you will use. So a blues progression in C will use a C blues scale for improvisation. If you just play the notes of that blues scale during a blues progression, from low to high, then back from high to low, it will sound great!

For a more interesting improvisation, apply some different rhythms to the blues scale as you play it up and down. Break each note into two parts, and apply the shuffle rhythm. Insert some beats or half beats of silence, or try playing three notes to a beat. Experiment!

Instead of playing the scale from one end to the other, try jumping from one note to one that is *not* next to it. Or choose two or three notes from the scale, and play different combinations of just those three notes.

Review the "Blues Tension Chart," and play! The I note of the scale will generally have the most relaxed feel, followed by the V note. The bV note will provide the most tense feel. The IV, bVII, and bIII notes will be somewhere in between, in less to more tense order. If you like, create a four or eight beat sequence of notes (called a **"riff"** or **"lick"**) and play it throughout the progression, as many times as it will fit in.

A fairly advanced but commonly used improvisation technique involves playing a blues scale from high end to low in the following way. Play each note, then the next lower note, then the original note again. Then go down one note, and do the same thing, as described for a key of C blues scale — it makes for a great, long riff, especially if you hold the last note!

C - Bb - C - Bb - G - Bb - G - Gb - G - Gb - F - Gb

F - Eb - F - Eb - C - Eb - C

Try doing that last sequence with one beat for each set of three notes (playing triplets), or use any rhythm that feels right to you. Make up similar ways of repeating notes of the scale.

Remember, since the I note is the most relaxed note of the scale, it is good to end a sequence of notes on the I. You may want to try different ways of ending up on the I note — I often like to finish a sequence with the notes bVII - VII - I (in C, that would be Bb - B - C). The VII note is not part of the blues scale, but it fits in well between the bVII and the I. Try playing the highest note of the scale in between each other note and ending with the ending just described, as (in C):

C - Bb - C - G - C - Gb - C - F - C - Eb - C - Bb - B - C

Play it one note per beat, add two beats of silence after the last note, and you've got a great bluesy/jazzy sounding four bar solo! Experiment with some four or eight beat licks that end on the V note — they will work well as turnarounds, when inserted in the last bar or two of the progression.

Which Scale to Use

If you want to improvise on a chord structure but are not sure what scale to use, just look at the chords used in the song. If they are mostly major, try improvising with notes from the major scale. If they are mostly minor, use the minor scale to improvise, and if there are lots of seventh chords, try a blues scale. The pentatonic scale can fit in lots of places, so it's always worth a try. The blues scale can also fit into many different chord structures, even non-blues structures, although it will always create "bluesy" sounding improvisations. But there's nothing wrong with that!

A Solo Suggestion

The previous suggestions for using scale improvisations all work fine, when played against a blues chord progression. But what happens when you want to play alone or "solo", without a chord progression to play against? In order to keep the feeling of the chord changes without actually playing any chords, you must provide hints of the progression, built right into your improvisations. It's not too hard to do.

Simply use any and all of the notes of the scale during the I chord parts of the verse, but make sure to use plenty of the I note of the scale. Emphasize the IV note of the scale during the IV chords, but don't neglect to use any of the other notes. Emphasize the V note of the scale during the V chords, along with any of the other notes that you have time to fit in.

If you really want to keep the chord structure obvious when improvising, use the root note (first note) of a chord as the note on which you *begin* any of your improvised work during a measure of that chord of the progression. In other words, use a IV note as the first note of any sequence of improvised notes you use during a bar of a IV chord. Use a V note to begin any of your improvised work during the V chord part of the progression.

Doing this allows you to play by yourself, but still maintain the feeling of the chord progression, by *implying* the chord structure. Especially for single note instruments, which cannot provide chords for themselves to play along with, this can be a wonderful way to play solo.

Combining Scale and Chord Notes

Another easy way to keep a chord progression clear, especially when playing by yourself, is to combine both the chord and scale approaches to improvisation. Play a bar of chord, then a bar of scale improvisation, but feel free to combine the chord and scale notes in any way that feels right to you.

Here is a very simple visual example. It's in blues form, so try to keep a shuffle rhythm on the chord parts. Notice how I depart from the "chord/note" bar pattern to follow a bar of G7 chord (the dominant part of my twelve bar) with a bar of F7 chord, instead of playing single notes for the second subdominant. Why? Because it felt right.... (slashes show beat)

```
\\\\        \    \    \    \      \\\\        \    \    \    \
C maj.      Eb   F    Gb   G      C maj.      G    Gb   F

\\\\        \    \    \    \      \\\\        \    \    \    \
F maj.      C    Bb   G    Gb     C maj.      Bb   G    Gb

\\\\   \\\\   \\\\      \      \    \    \
 G7    F7    C maj.     G    F    Gb   G
```

Just Playing...

After you've spent a bit of time practicing some of the techniques described above, try forgetting about them! Turn your backing music up high, and the lights down low, try to clear your mind of any thoughts, and just play. See what comes out. As master saxophonist Charlie "Bird" Parker said, "First you master your instrument, then you master the music, then you forget about all that...and just play."

I include a section on what you might call "playing without thinking" in all of my instrumental instruction books. For many people, it really works — so try..."Just Playing!"!

Composing Songs

There are four main elements to consider when composing your own songs: lyrics, melody, rhythm, and chord structure. The last three are terms that we have already discussed. **"Lyrics"** are just the words of a song.

In some ways, creating a song is somewhat like creating an improvisation. Composing is more complex, though, because when improvising, we have already chosen an existing song structure and can then easily figure out which scale and basic rhythm to use. When composing a song from scratch, we have much more freedom, and also many more decisions to make. We need to decide what musical style we want our song to be in, then choose a chord structure and a scale to use. The choice of scale will be very dependent on the "feel" or mood of our song, so it often pays to start with the concept or central idea of the song, and at least some of the lyrics.

Starting With the Lyrics

Once we have a central idea that we want to express, we need lyrics — Words! Since some of the words of a song often rhyme, an idea and two rhyming words can often be the basis of an entire song. The idea of a summer romance added to the words Moon and June, the feeling of sadness for a lost love plus Yesterday and Away, a sense of awe plus the words Night and Bright — the possibilities are endless.

Perhaps you have a feeling or idea you would like to express. Can you think of some sets of rhyming words to illustrate that idea? If so, you're on!

Chord Structure and Rhythm

Now that you have an idea and a few rhymes, any of the chord structures in this book can be used to write a song. It just depends on what style you would like your song to be in. Choosing the twelve bar blues structure with a shuffle rhythm as a framework on which to place your lyrics will make your song tend to sound like a blues. If you choose the rock rhythm and rock variation of the blues structure, your song will sound like rock and roll. Choosing an eight bar country structure will give your song a C & W feel.

It's really your choice — most lyrics can be added to any of the chord structures. Of course, the way in which the lyrics will be fit to the structure is different. I will illustrate how the same rhyming words and idea can be used in very different situations, by using a song I've recently written (originally as a C & W piece). But I'll present it as both a country song, and as a blues, so that you can see how I fit the same words into two different chord structures.

The Twelve Bar Blues Song

In a blues progression, three lines with rhyming words at the end are usually divided up between the twelve bars, four bars to each line, with a beat or two of silence in the middle of each line. Often, the first and second lines are the same, so each verse requires only two rhyming words.

If you listen to some blues songs, and consider the advice and example on this page, you will be able to write a simple blues song of your own, and fit it to the blues chord structure:

I - I - I - I - IV - IV - I - I - V7 - IV - I - V7

Observe how I fit my lyrics to the twelve bar blues structure (chord symbols under each line). Notice that the first few words *begin* before the first I chord — these are known as **"pick up"** notes or words, and occur during the last beat of the last chord of the introduction. They are technically part of the turn-around (count beat slashes throughout the song if you don't believe me) — That's why they have a V7 chord symbol under them.

Also notice the long "breaks" between lyric lines. During these breaks, and the shorter breaks between lines, I apply some harmonica "riffs" (also called "fills"), to fill up the space.

You'll also see that I break some one syllable words (like "he-ad") into two parts — This is a great place to use two blues scale notes (like Vb and IV), in traditional blues lyric fashion!

```
 \           \   \    \          \  \
There's no dent in the pillow...
 V7          I


              \        \     \    \  \\\\\\
           where your he-ad used to lie...


 \          \   \    \          \  \
There's no dent in the pillow...
           IV


              \        \     \    \  \\\\\\
           where your he-ad used to lie...
                                     I


 \         \        \   \      \       \
Saddest thing I've ever seen...
          V7                          IV7


              \        \        \    \  \\\  \\\
           and it made me want to cry.
                                I           V7
```

The C & W Eight Bar Song

In the country eight bar chord structure (page 53), two sets of rhyming words would probably be divided into four lines of two bars each, like this:

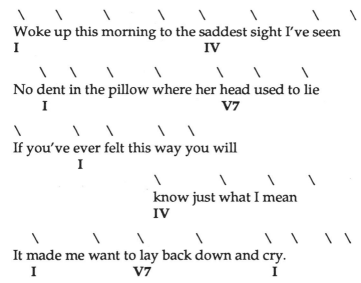

\   \   \   \   \   \   \   \
Woke up this morning to the saddest sight I've seen
I   IV

\   \   \   \   \   \   \
No dent in the pillow where her head used to lie
   I   V7

\   \   \   \   \
If you've ever felt this way you will
    I

                   \   \   \   \
                   know just what I mean
                   IV

\   \   \   \   \   \   \ \
It made me want to lay back down and cry.
  I   V7   I

Of course, you can create your own chord structures and fit lyrics to them, too. Begin by working with I, IV, and V7 chords, after re-reading the sections on folk and pop music use of these chords. Good luck!

Melody

The melody, or tune, of a song is one of its most important components. In fact, sometimes a song composer will think of a melody first, then write lyrics. Creating a melody is like improvising. Just use my suggestions for scale improvisation to put notes together that you like, in a rhythm pattern you like.

Choosing notes from the major scale, and putting them together in various combinations, will provide a more cheerful or happy feel. Choosing notes from the minor scale will provide a plaintive feel — the minor scale is what gives songs like *Greensleeves*, *Summertime*, and *Autumn Leaves* their wistful air. Choosing notes from the blues scale will give a, well, bluesy feel.

Experiment with some melody creation. Play the scale that you think will best fit the lyrics or idea that you have (for example, a minor scale would probably not fit a happy song about Friday afternoon) a few times. Then try different note combinations, singing the lyrics as you play the notes.

After you have worked with each scale, you may want to try to combine them. Make up a major scale melody for a mostly happy set of lyrics, but if there is a slightly wistful or tense feeling in one part of the words, insert a note from the minor or blues scale that isn't in the major scale, during that word. This is something that you learn by doing, so listen to songs that you like, buy songbooks, and try it yourself!

Jazz Chord Structures

I would like to end this book with a very brief look at some of the most complicated styles of making music. Jazz, and certain pop and rock songs, use more complex chords and chord structures than the other styles that we have been studying up to now. A complete study of these complex styles would fill many books, so I will just attempt to give you a general idea of advanced chord and scale usage.

Most of the advanced chord changes are based on three music theory concepts: the **"circle of fifths"** or the **"II - V -I"** chords or **"chromatic scale movement"**, as I will illustrate in the following sections. **"Substitutions"** for the more basic I, IV, and V chords that we already studied are also used.

Twelve Bar Jazz/Blues

By substituting more varied chords for the I, IV and V, we can "jazz up" our old friend the twelve bar blues progression. We've already tried some chord substitutions, as when we changed the IV to another V7 in the rock twelve bar, or when we changed some I and IV chords to I7 and IV7 chords.

A full study of chord substitution would take hundreds, if not thousands, of pages. But I would like to give you one example, that happens to be one of my favorite versions of the blues progression. As you read the next few pages, you will understand why I made the substitutions that I did.

For a really jazzy minor blues progression, you can substitute one bar of #iv (sharped minor fourth) in the place of the expected iv chord in the sixth measure. This sixth measure, of course, is the second measure of the first subdominant (page 51). So now you know what I meant on the back cover of this book, when I said, "Let's play a minor twelve bar with a sharped four in the second measure of the subdominant!"

I have also changed the usual V7 - iv of the ninth and tenth bars into a ii7 (two minor 7) - V7, and used the more exciting two bar i/iv - i/V7 turnaround.

i - iv - i - i - iv - #iv - i - i - ii7 - V7 - i/iv - i/V7

Please compare the above minor blues, with substitutions, to the simplest possible minor blues, with no substitutions (except for using minor chords in the place of the original major chords) that I introduced on page 52, below.

i - iv - i - i - iv - iv - i - i - V7 - iv - i - V7

If you can play them together, you'll hear quite a bit of difference — One sounds a lot "jazzier!"

The Circle of Fifths

The circle of fifths really isn't a circle at all. It's just a way of referring to an interesting musical fact. If you begin on any note, C for instance, and then jump up to the V note of C (which is G), then jump up to the V note of G (which is D), and keep jumping up to the next V note — eventually you will get back to C, like this (written first with #'s, then b's):

C - G - D - A - E - B - F# - C# - G# - D# - A# - F - C

C - G - D - A - E - B - Gb - Db - Ab - Eb - Bb - F - C

What's so important about that? Well, it sounds good when you play all or part of this chord sequence from *right to left*, for some reason. Jazz composers (and lots of pop composers) like to take three or four chord sequences from the circle of fifths, and insert them into jazz or pop chord structures.

So select a three note sequence from the circle of fifths, like C - G -D. Now play the notes from right to left (that's the way circle of fifths sequences need to be played), as D - G - C. They just seem to "sound right together," as you can easily hear.

Now let's assign roman numeral names to the notes of the circle of fifths, using C as the I.

I - V - II - VI - III - VII - IV# - I# - V# -II# - VI# - IV - I

Certain sequences, like (from right to left, with lines) II - V - I and III - VI - II - V, are *crucial* to jazz.

The II - V - I Jazz Chord Sequence

If you take any three chords that are next to each other (like C - G - D) from the circle of fifths, and assign the leftmost one the roman numeral I (C = I), you'll find that the G is then a V, and the D is then a II.

When you play them from right to left (the way it sounds good), you get a D - G - C, or **II - V - I**, progression. And the II - V - I progression is one of the most popular chord sequences in jazz music. Why? Because it just sounds good. And that's why I used it in the ninth, tenth, and first half of the eleventh bars of my favorite minor twelve bar, above!

Chromatic Chord Movement

This term refers to the fact that playing a series of chords based on the notes that are next to each other in the chromatic scale always sounds good. Sometimes up to six or seven chords are used, but usually a chromatic chord movement involves only two, three or four chords, like C - B - Bb - A, or F - F# - G. Many jazz and pop composers use this type of chord sequence in their songs. It's why I used a IV - #IV substitution in my minor blues — Worked, didn't it?

The Theory Behind a Rock "Bridge"

Chromatic movement that *skips* a chromatic scale note can also work quite well, although usually the last two chords in such a sequence are chromatic notes that are right next to each other (in other words, the last movement does not skip a step).

You can illustrate this by using chords based on the chromatic notes C - B - Bb - A - Ab - G, and then skipping the B and A notes.

C - B - Bb - A - Ab - G

C -   - Bb -   - Ab - G

This gives you the chord structure C - Bb - Ab - G, which goes down by skipping chromatic steps, except for the last two (which are next to each other in the chromatic scale). It's the exact (I - bVII - bVI - V) progression used as the "bridge" in Del Shannon's rock classic *Runaway*, and many other songs.

I - bVII - bVI - V   **C - Bb - Ab - G**

Harmonica virtuoso Norton Buffalo does an incredible solo using this bridge on the Bonnie Raitt cover of *Runaway*. His secret? He uses four different harmonicas, one for each chord, and plays blues scale riffs based on the C blues scale during the C chord, the Bb blues scale during the Bb chord, the Ab blues scale during the Ab chord, and the G blues scale during the G chord. Try it some time, on any instrument!

32 Bar Jazz AABA Chord Structure

After the twelve bar structure, the most popular jazz chord structure is the **32 bar "AABA"** progression. Each letter, A, A, B, and A, represents *not a key* but one eight bar (8 x 4 = 32) part of the progression. Three of these portions are the same: the three A pieces, natch. The B part (called a "bridge" or "chorus") is different.

There are literally an infinity of variations on the 32 bar AABA structure. However, if you learn even the simplest, many of the others will sound familiar. The following is one of the most basic variations.

Each eight bar A part starts with a bar of I chord followed by two sets of II - V - I chord combinations. Here's a *simplified* version of the first five bars of the A part of an AABA jazz progression (to help you see the II - V - I chord sections more clearly).

I - II/V7 - I - II/V7 - I

But the real II - V - I chords used are *actually* the scarier looking II minor 7 to V7 to I chords (perhaps the most common jazz use of the II - V - I), like this:

I - IIm7/V7 - I - IIm7/V7 - I

The last three bars of each eight bar A section are made up of a chromatic motion part (in bars six and seven, from IV to #IV to V7) which finally "resolves" (see page 43 if you need to) back to a bar of I.

IV/#IV - V7 - I

Put the first five bars together with the last three bars to get the entire eight bar A part:

I - IIm7/V7 - I - IIm7/V7 - I - IV/#IV - V7 - I

The eight bar B part is nothing more than a set of four circle of fifths chords, III - VI - II - V, with each chord played for two bars (and the V changed to V7).

III - III - VI - VI - II - II - V7 - V7

Take three of the A parts, and put them together with one of the B parts, in AABA order. This is what you get, in roman numerals, and in the key of C.

A: **I - IIm7/V7 - I - IIm7/V7 - I - IV/#IV - V7 - I**

A: **I - IIm7/V7 - I - IIm7/V7 - I - IV/#IV - V7 - I**

B: **III - III - VI - VI - II - II - V7 - V7**

A: **I - IIm7/V7 - I - IIm7/V7 - I - IV/#IV - V7 - I**

A: **C - Dm7/G7 - C - Dm7/G7 - C - F/#F - G7 - C**

A: **C - Dm7/G7 - C - Dm7/G7 - C - F/#F - G7 - C**

B: **E - E - A - A - D - D - G7 - G7**

A: **C - Dm7/G7 - C - Dm7/G7 - C - F/#F - G7 - C**

Simplest AABA Jazz Improvisation

There are *many* ways to improvise with this chord structure. More sophisticated players (more sophisticated than me, at least) might use as many as six or so different modes or scales to accompany an AABA — Using a different scale for each chord in the structure.

But you don't need to do anything that fancy to sound good. In the 32 bar key of C example I gave, for instance, you can use a C blues scale to improvise during all of the "A" parts. This means, of course, that you can use a blues scale based on the I note no matter what specific key you choose to create a 32 bar progression in. Playing the 32 bar "changes" in Eb? Just use an Eb blues scale during all of the A parts.

The blues scale based on the I chord will work perfectly during the I chord measures of the A part. It will work very well during the V7 measures and half measures. It'll work okay during the IIm7 parts, but you might throw in a II note here (like a D note in the key of C) for a beat or half a beat, to sound "righter".

What to Do On the Jazz Bridge

The B part, or bridge, is a bit trickier. Of course the I based blues scale will work well during the V7 part of the bridge. But it won't work too well for improvising during III or VI or II parts of the bridge.

I suggest using Norton Buffalo's technique: Play a blues scale based on the III during the III chords, a blues scale based on the VI during the VI parts, and a blues scale based on the II during the II chords of the bridge. Then you can either use a blues scale based on the V chord or return to the I based blues scale for the last two bars of the bridge.

Now you're back in the last A part, and your I based blues scale will work just fine again! And you only had to learn the blues scale in four different keys (in C: C, D, E, and A) to do it!

To sum up a very simple blues scale improvisng strategy for 32 bar AABA jazz chord structures, using blues scales only:

Use blues scale based on the:	(roman)	(key of C)
For all of the A parts:	I	C
For B Part, III chord:	III	E
For B Part, VI chord:	VI	A
For B Part, II chord:	II	D
For B Part, V7 chord:	V or I	G or C

More Advanced Jazz Chords

Jazz sometimes uses unusual chords to substitute for the major, minor, seventh, and minor seventh chords that we've been using. The study of the use of these chords is beyond the scope of this little book, but I would like to show you how to construct four of the most often-used of these chords, so that if you see them in a chord chart, you will know what to do.

major sixth chord (M6) = I - III - V - VI.

minor sixth chord (m6) = I - bIII - V - VI

major seventh chord (M7) = I - III - V - VII

half diminished seventh chord (ø7) = I - bIII - bV - bVII

Jazz players often use five to seven note chords, that include "ninths," "elevenths," and "thirteenths." A ninth note is the same as a II note, but one octave higher. An eleventh is the same as a IV, an octave higher. A thirteenth is the same as a VI, an octave up.

So a C13 chord might be played as: C - E - G - D - F - A. These are called "superimposed" chords, and like so much of jazz, outside the scope of this book.

Where The Modes Came From

Here is how the modes or modal scales were created, back in the experimental days after Pythagoras. Though this information won't really help you to play, it seems to be included in every music theory curriculum, and does clarify how the minor, dorian, and myxolydian modes relate to the major scale.

The seven notes that would come to be called the major scale, or major mode, were chosen out of the twelve notes of the chromatic scale. These seven major notes were picked because they had been created using simpler ratios (see page 14) than the other five. Some say that these seven notes had actually been in use before the chromatic scale was developed. In any event, these seven notes that were to become known worldwide as the major scale (bottom) represented a simplification of the twelve note chromatic scale (top).

C	C#	D	D#	E	F	F#	G	G#	A	A#	B	C
C		D		E	F		G		A		B	C

At some point (conceptually if not literally), two major scales were placed end to end, to form two octaves worth of sound. I will write them down as two C major scales, even though letter names for notes had not yet been invented.

C D E F G A B C D E F G A B C

Then, instead of playing the notes of the major scale from C to C, for instance, the notes from D to the next D were tried by some unknown genius.

	C D E F G A B C D E F G A B C
Dorian:	D E F G A B C D
Myxolydian:	G A B C D E F G
Aeolian (minor):	A B C D E F G A

This was called the **"dorian mode,"** and it is a popular jazz improvising scale to this day. Then the notes from E to the next E were played ("phrygian mode"), the notes from F to F ("lydian mode"), and so on. The modal scale based on G, the fifth note of the major scale became the **"myxolydian mode,"** still a popular improvising scale. And the modal scale based on the sixth note of the major scale, called the **"aeolian mode,"** became our present day minor scale!

More Jazz Modes and Scales

Jazz music uses many more scales than any other type of music, although the major, the minor, and especially the blues scale can be used to improvise jazz, as I've just discussed. Once again, use of these advanced scales is beyond the scope of this book, but I will write some of them out for you.

The **dorian** mode or scale is somewhat like a compromise between the blues and the minor scale. It works quite well with minor seventh chords, and looks like this, in roman numerals and in C:

I - II - bIII - IV - V - VI - bVII - I

C - D - Eb - F - G - A - Bb - C

The **myxolydian** mode is somewhat like a cross between the major and the blues scale. It works well as a less bluesy alternative to the blues scale when used with seventh chords (it fits in perfectly with them), and looks like:

I - II - III - IV - V - VI - bVII - I

C - D - E - F - G - A - Bb - C

There are also two variations on the minor scale that are sometimes used in jazz. The **melodic minor**, which is played *only* when going in a low note to high note direction, fits well with the minor sixth chord, and uses the notes:

I - II - bIII - IV - V - VI - VII - I

C - D - Eb - F - G - A - B - C

The **harmonic minor** also works with minor sixths:

I - II - bIII - IV - V - bVI - VII - I

C - D - Eb - F - G - Ab - B - C

The **whole tone scale** has an unearthly sound, and it fits into many jazz improvisations, if skillfully used. It fits in especially well when used with half diminished chords. In roman numeral and C, it looks like:

I - II - III - #IV - #V - #VI - I

C - D - E - F# - G# - A# - C

Practice playing these scales if you like jazz, and consider buying the jazz improv books that I recommend below — They have more detail on scale use.

And if these scales seem intimidating, remember that the blues scale can be used with many jazz structures, as I have already described for the 32 bar AABA. You may not sound really "far out," but you won't sound wrong!

Where to Go for More

For more information on jazz theory I would suggest Jerry Coker's *Improvising Jazz* (Prentice-Hall, 1964), and Daniel Ricigliano's *Popular and Jazz Harmony* (Donato, 1969). These books are not easy, but reading *this* book will have prepared you to brave the jungle of more advanced music theory.

Appendices

On Reading Music

Yes, learning to read standard notation takes time and commitment. But it is a great way to be able to play anything that anybody else has ever played, and that's saying a lot. Until I come out with a book on it, Howard Shanet's *Learn To Read Music* (Simon & Shuster, 1956) is a good, simple place to start.

Why Keyboard, Why Guitar?

As I've said before, if you are a vocalist, or if you play a single note instrument, learning to play even a little keyboard or guitar can really help you to master music theory. If keyboard appeals to you, I suggest getting a low cost programmable electronic keyboard, such as the Yamaha PSS-480 (under $150 new). If you'd like to experiment with guitar, my *Instant Guitar* method allows you to play simple folk, blues, and rock chord structures such as the ones described here within an hour or so. Details? Please see page 78.

How to Play Confidently With Other Musicians

There are four pieces of advice that will allow you to play confidently with other musicians: Know the Language, Be Honest About Your Abilities, Observe Jamming Etiquette, and When In Doubt — Sit Out.

Know the Language

As I said on the back cover, music theory is a language. If you want to play with other musicians, you must know what they are talking about. Make sure you understand the terms tonic, subdominant, and dominant, the letter names of notes, the names of chord types, roman numeral names for chords, the difference between a chorus and a verse — all stuff that I've covered in this book. It's especially important to know how to read — and write — simple chord charts: **Scrawling out a copy of the "changes" for each player has saved many a jamm session!**

If you know that you are going to be playing a specific type of music, like blues, or country, know both the roman numeral names for the common chord structures, and memorize a few specific key chord structures as well. Keyboard players will often want to play in C or G, and guitar players in E and A, especially if they aren't too experienced, so these are good keys to know. It's also a good idea to memorize the I, IV, and V chords in every key, since these are the chords most likely to occur.

If a song is suggested that is not a chord structure that you know, ask someone (if there is time) to run the chords down for you (bass or keyboard players are best to ask, since drummers and vocalists may not think in terms of chords). A strange seeming structure may be simply a variation on one you already know.

For example, blues are sometimes (though not too often) played in an eight or sixteen bar format instead of the usual twelve. The rhythm, and the blues scale, are the same. So if you just realize that the chords come in a different order, you're set, after a listen or two! For your information, here are the two most common eight and sixteen bar blues variations:

I - I - I - I - I - I - I - I - IV - IV - I - I - V7 - IV - I - V7

I - V7 - IV7 - IV7 - I - V7 - I/IV7 - I/V7

Be Honest About Your Abilities

There are many different jamming situations. If possible, begin your jamming career by playing with friends or acquaintances in a private place, not a club or bar. Be open about your level of ability, and make sure they are willing to play what you can do, at least some of the time. If not, you probably shouldn't be playing with them at all.

Open mike (microphone) nights at clubs, especially those with a house band to back up the amateur players, usually expect a certain minimum degree of competence. That's the bad news. The good news is that they will usually be willing to play exactly what you want play. So inquire first if the backup band will play your request, then make sure that you're decided on a style and key of music. Ask for it, then jamm!

Observe Jamming Etiquette

Unfortunately, there is no Emily Post or Miss Manners to tell you just how to behave when playing with other people. So here are a few tips.

Perhaps most important is that it's better to play too little than too much. If you are asked to sit in, try not to insert your playing into every second of the song. Let the other musicians ask you to play more, not less. Be especially careful about playing when a vocalist is singing, or when another instrumentalist is taking a "solo" or "lead" (that is, creating an improvisation, which is usually done one musician at a time).

Face the audience, and look interested, even if you're not playing at the moment. Before playing, find out who the group leader is, and ask them for a signal if they want you to take a solo. Watch the leader closely, as he or she will often signal by hand or body language that one of the players should solo, or that everyone should be silent for a few beats, or exactly when to end a piece.

When in Doubt, Sit out

Be sensitive to whether the other musicians want you to sit in, or not. Professional bands are often nervous about having amateurs play along on their paying gigs, so never force yourself on an unenthusiastic pro band. Wait instead for an open mike, or a jamm session in a private home.

And if you aren't sure you know a song, even if you have been sitting in successfully, have the sense to sit that one out. As the old saying goes, "When in doubt, sit out."

Playing With Other Amateurs

When you're playing with other musicians of your level or below, in a casual setting, please share your knowledge of music theory with them. Suggest writing out chord charts for each player, especially if attempting something that not everyone knows. It can be much easier to play together, if everyone knows just what to do. When you find yourself one of the more experienced or better trained musicians in a group (and this humble book may go a surprisingly long way towards putting you in that situation), it's your responsibility to help other players who may be less competent.

Because for me, co-operation is a big part of the satisfaction that I get from making music with other people. Helping a group of musicians, no matter what their level of expertise, to make better music is far more gratifying than proving how good I am. The "whole becomes greater than the sum of its parts" — if the parts help to make it so.

And you can help, by learning to be the best musician that you can be. With your new understanding of music theory, you'll raise the technical and enjoyment level of any jamm session!

— David Harp

Sales Pitch

I apologize if it seems as though I've been relentlessly pitching my various other products throughout this book. Yet if you have enjoyed this book, and found it to be of value, you may want to read about some of my other instructional products. I'm proud to say that many thousands of you who have read *Music Theory Made Easy* have gone on to use my other music methods for harmonica, percussion, flute, or guitar!

New: Music Theory Book...with CD

We now have a new 3rd edition (the book that you're holding is the 2nd edition) of *Music Theory Made Easy*. We understand that some folks like to learn by reading — that's why we are keeping this edition in print.

But for those who like to listen to examples while they read, the new edition comes with a 74 minute instructional CD. Each section of the book is related to a track on the CD which provides a musical example of what I'm writing about in that part of the book.

The new book is a bit larger (6" wide, not 4.5") so it includes about 25% more information — much of it on improvisation — plus a 74 minute CD! The 80 page Book and the 74 minute CD together are only $12.95.

NEW! David's 74 Min. Playalong CD

Mainly for harmonica players but useable with *any* instrument, this CD has 74 minutes of various styles of blues & rock playalong music. Mostly in key of G, some tracks in E and C. It's **$8.95** by itself, or *add* it to any other item in your order and *Save $2* — pay only **$6.95**!)

The Instant Rhythm Kit

This 64 page book and 60 minute tape go much deeper into the study of rhythm than my *Music Theory* book. Learn rock backbeats, blues shuffles, jazz grooves, plus lots of Latin and African rhythms! It's fun and an easy way to learn to read standard rhythm notation. Great for kids or adults. Book and tape only $12.95, with set of beginner's drumsticks $14.95 (while they last!)

Instant Guitar

Are you a singer, or would-be songwriter? Then you *need* to be able to play a "chord" instrument — ASAP! *Instant Guitar* (80 page book, 98 minute tape) features the unique "Chord-Snaffle™," my simple but effective invention that lets you play chords *with only one finger!* You'll play *simplified* blues, rock, folk, country, new age, and even jazz in less than an hour! For beginners *only*. Book, tape, & "Snaffle" just $14.95.

www.davidharp.com or *www.bluesharp.com*

Blues & Rock Harp "Positions" Made Easy!

Blues & Rock Harp "Positions" Made Easy is the first book on music theory just for harp players! "Positions" are the way harp players describe what key (C or A or F etc.) harmonica to use when playing different kinds of music. Includes hundreds of great scales and riffs, some easy enough for beginners, some hard enough for pros! 96 pp, $6.95.

NEW! LOW COST HARPS IN ALL KEYS $6 EACH!

Make Me Musical™ Kid's Harmonica!

Make Me Musical Harmonica Video Can't miss method for kids from 4 to 9! Blues, rock, folk, classical, lots of fun & costumes! It's short and sweet (just 33 minutes) but even young ones are often riveted by my super-simple Harmonica Hand Signal Method™ ! Only $16.95 with 24 page song and riff booklet and key of C harmonica! Available soon in DVD!

3 Minutes to™ Flute

The versatility and pure tone of the "fipple flute" or "tin whistle" will surprise anyone who thinks it's "not a serious musical instrument." This 80 page book & 74 minute playalong CD teaches blues, rock, folk, jazz, and Celtic songs in notation so easy you'll be playing within minutes — guaranteed! With two chromatic octave, key of D, "Clarke" brand tin flute, only $16.95.

3 Minutes to Blues, Rock, & Folk Harmonica

Carry a band in your pocket — where ever you go! This 96 page book and 74 minute self-guided playalong CD will teach you a whole variety of harp styles — in minutes! The new 3rd edition is as user-friendly as any instruction method I've ever created! The book and CD alone are $9.95. With a Mojo Deluxe key of C harmonica, just $15.95.

The Three Minute Meditator (New 5th Ed.)

Some call this the most user-friendly book on meditation ever! New edition is better than ever, by David and his twin Dr. Nina Smiley. 256 pages, $12.95.

Instant Blues Harmonica

9th Totally Revised Edition!

If you've enjoyed the 12 Bar Blues info in this book, you'll love my blues and rock harmonica method! This newest blues/rock improv package is perfect for total beginners — you'll start improvising right away! It's also perfect for more experienced harp players who have mostly taught themselves to play, and never really learned about blues chords or scales. Learn to create your own 12 Bar Blues and Rock improvisations, then apply your new skills to other instruments! This is our most popular method ever (we have thousands of letters from satisfied customers). 80 page book and 74 minute "self-guided" CD only $12.95. With a key of C harp, only $17.95.

The Pocket Harmonica Songbook!

A "sampler" harp book with over 40 great songs in all styles, arranged for beginner to intermediate players, just $6.95! And we also have lots of **more advanced harmonica instruction methods!**